Finding Pathways

Social scientists have identified a need to move beyond the analysis of correlation among variables to the study of causal mechanisms that link them. Nicholas Weller and Jeb Barnes propose that a solution lies in "pathway analysis": the use of case studies to explore the causal links between related variables. This book focuses on how the small-N component of multi-method research can meaningfully contribute and add value to the study of causal mechanisms. The authors present both an extended rationale for the unique role that case studies can play in causal mechanism research, and a detailed view of the types of knowledge that case studies should try to generate and how to leverage existing large-N data to guide the case selection process. The authors explain how to use their approach both to select cases and to provide context on previously studied cases.

Nicholas Weller is Assistant Professor of Political Science and International Relations at the University of Southern California.

Jeb Barnes is Associate Professor of Political Science at the University of Southern California.

Strategies for Social Inquiry

Finding Pathways: Mixed-Method Research for Studying
Causal Mechanisms

Editors

Colin Elman, *Maxwell School of Syracuse University*
John Gerring, *Boston University*
James Mahoney, *Northwestern University*

Editorial board

Bear Braumoeller, David Collier, Francesco Guala, Peter Hedström, Theodore
Hopf, Uskali Maki, Rose McDermott, Charles Ragin, Theda Skocpol, Peter
Spiegler, David Waldner, Lisa Wedeen, Christopher Winship

This new book series presents texts on a wide range of issues bearing upon the
practice of social inquiry. Strategies are construed broadly to embrace the full
spectrum of approaches to analysis, as well as relevant issues in philosophy of
social science.

Published Titles

John Gerring, *Social Science Methodology: A Unified Framework, 2nd edition*
Michael Coppedge, *Democratization and Research Methods*
Thad Dunning, *Natural Experiments in the Social Sciences: A Design-Based
    Approach*
Carsten Q. Schneider and Claudius Wagemann, *Set-Theoretic Methods for the
    Social Sciences: A Guide to Qualitative Comparative Analysis*

Forthcoming titles

Andrew Bennett and Jeffrey T. Checkel, *Process Tracing in the Social Sciences:
    From Metaphor to Analytic Tool*
Diana Kapiszewski, Lauren M. MacLean and Benjamin L. Read, *Field Research
    in Political Science: Practices and Principles*
Jason Seawright, *Multi-Method Social Science: Combining Qualitative and
    Quantitative Tools*
Peter Spiegler, *A Constructive Critique of Economic Modeling*

Finding Pathways

Mixed-Method Research for Studying
Causal Mechanisms

Nicholas Weller

Department of Political Science and School of International Relations
University of Southern California

Jeb Barnes

Department of Political Science
University of Southern California

CAMBRIDGE
UNIVERSITY PRESS

CAMBRIDGE
UNIVERSITY PRESS

University Printing House, Cambridge CB2 8BS, United Kingdom

Cambridge University Press is part of the University of Cambridge.

It furthers the University's mission by disseminating knowledge in the pursuit of
education, learning and research at the highest international levels of excellence.

www.cambridge.org
Information on this title: www.cambridge.org/9781107684768

© Nicholas Weller and Jeb Barnes 2014

This publication is in copyright. Subject to statutory exception
and to the provisions of relevant collective licensing agreements,
no reproduction of any part may take place without the written
permission of Cambridge University Press.

First published 2014

Printed by CPI Group (UK) Ltd, Croydon CR0 4YY

A catalogue record for this publication is available from the British Library

ISBN 978-1-107-04106-6 Hardback
ISBN 978-1-107-68476-8 Paperback

Additional resources for this publication at www.cambridge.org/weller-barnes

Cambridge University Press has no responsibility for the persistence or accuracy of
URLs for external or third-party internet websites referred to in this publication,
and does not guarantee that any content on such websites is, or will remain,
accurate or appropriate.

Contents

Figures

Tables

Acknowledgments

This project began as a conversation in Nick's office. We were advising a number of graduate students who planned to combine qualitative and quantitative research in their dissertations. The students wanted to use various types of large-N analyses to establish associations between variables and then use case studies to investigate the processes that connected these variables. The idea sounded promising, but the details of how to use multi-method research to probe the links between variables were somewhat vague. At the time, we thought that it might be fun and useful to write a short article on this subject. We soon realized, however, that this topic could not be contained in a single article, and we began the journey of writing a book on what has proven to be an enormously complex subject.

This journey has been supported by a group of wonderful scholars and colleagues. It is our pleasure to thank them for all of their support, insights, and patience, as well as to absolve them of any mistakes that remain in the final version of this work. First, at Cambridge University Press, we would like to thank our editor, John Haslam, his assistant, Carrie Parkinson, and the anonymous reviewers, whose comments greatly improved the manuscript. A special debt is owed to the acquisition editors for the series on Strategies for Social Inquiry, Colin Elman, Jim Mahoney, and especially John Gerring. These three not only advocated for the book but also provided us invaluable opportunities to participate in the research workshop at the Institute for Qualitative and Multi-Method Research at the Maxwell School of Public Policy at Syracuse University. We also thank Joanna North and Lila Stromer for their copyediting assistance.

Second, many scholars were extremely generous in responding to earlier drafts and offering insights. We are especially grateful to Adam Glynn, who commented on several iterations of conference papers, Jake Bowers, Diana Kapiszewski, and Gerry Munck, who served as discussants at a workshop on the manuscript, and Jane Junn, who tirelessly read drafts at various stages of the project. All of these fine scholars went above and beyond the call of duty and pushed us to produce a much better book. If there was an All Star team for colleagues, they would be in the starting lineup. We also thank our colleagues at the University of Southern California who attended the workshop on the manuscript, including Tony Bertelli, Dennis Chong, Ann Crigler, Ben Graham, Christian Grose, Diana O'Brien, Brian Rathbun, and Jeffrey Sellers. Their participation and comments were greatly appreciated. We are grateful to Justin Berry and Mariano Bertucci for their research assistance.

Third, we would like to thank the Center for International Studies at USC (CIS), its director, Patrick James, and Indira Persad. At a critical point in the process – after the basic ideas for the book had started to take shape but before they were set in stone – we wanted to convene a group of scholars to comment on the manuscript. CIS generously provided funding and the administrative support for this workshop, which turned out to be critical in the project's development. We cannot thank them enough.

Finally, we would like to thank our cherished families, whose kindness, patience, and support allowed us to make this journey in the first place. We dedicate this book to them.

1 Pathway analysis and the elusive search for causal mechanisms

1.1 The allure of mixed-method research in the search for causal mechanisms

Scholars of judicial behavior have found time and time again an association between US Supreme Court justices' political ideologies and their votes (e.g., Pritchett 1948; Rhode and Spaeth 1976; Schubert 1965; Segal and Cover 1989; Segal et al. 1995; Segal and Spaeth 1993, 1999, 2002). Scholars differ sharply, however, over the meaning of this finding. Behavioralists argue that the relationship between ideology and votes suggests that justices largely ignore the law and impose their personal preferences when deciding cases. "Simply put, Rehnquist votes the way he does because he is extremely conservative; Marshall voted the way he did because he is extremely liberal" (Segal and Spaeth 1993: 65). Postbehavioralists envisage a very different decision-making process (Gillman 2001). They argue that justices begin with a good faith understanding of legal rules and principles, and that those general legal principles meaningfully constrain justices' discretion (e.g., Burton 1992; Gillman 1993, 1996; Cushman 1998; see also Dworkin 1978). From this perspective, conservative and liberal judges can end up voting quite differently from one another while still applying the same legal principle, just as two sergeants ordered to choose the "best" five soldiers from a platoon might both follow the order but still select different soldiers (Dworkin 1978).[1]

---

[1] This is a highly stylized account of what is admittedly a much richer and more nuanced debate (see, e.g., Epstein et al. 2013; Baum 1997, 2006). The goal is not to

In this area, the debate is not about the core findings of the quantitative research, but instead concerns the unobserved processes that link the critical explanatory variable and the outcome. In other words, the question is not *whether* ideology affects judicial votes, but *how* it does so. In the words of Howard Gillman (2001: 487), postbehavioralists

do not reject behavioralist descriptions of decision-making patterns, but they insist that behavioralists should not infer that these patterns mean an absence of legal motivations unless they have additional independent evidence that judges are basing their decisions on considerations that are not warranted by law.

This debate might seem technical but it is not a dusty, academic quibble, because it goes to the heart of questions about the rule of law in US Supreme Court decision-making. If individual justices start with specific policy outcomes in mind and apply the law instrumentally to fit their ideological preferences, then the ideal of the rule of law seems badly eroded. By contrast, if justices begin with good faith understandings of the law and legal precedents, which are often open-ended (like the order to choose the five "best" soldiers), and apply these principles consistently without regard to outcome but in light of very different (but sincerely held) political values, then the association between political ideology and votes might be less troubling because the law meaningfully guides judicial behavior, even if it fails to mechanically constrain judicial discretion or eliminate ideological splits on the Court. Under these circumstances, understanding the links between justices' ideology and their votes matters, and researchers need a strategy for exploring these unobserved processes.

This challenge is not limited to the judicial behavior literature. As we will see, the question of how an explanatory factor causes an outcome is central to a variety of research agendas. Comparative politics

summarize this vast and contested area. It is merely to give the reader a reference for the type of problem and research we are interested in addressing in this book.

scholars have been investigating the underlying links between natural resource wealth and both internal conflicts and low levels of democracy (discussed in Chapters 4, 6, and 7). International relations scholars are interested in how policies diffuse from one state to another, such as how the adoption of liberal economic policies in one state might affect the adoption of similar policies in other states (discussed in Chapter 5). Health policy scholars have long sought to understand how socio-economic status (SES) influences health outcomes (discussed in Chapter 8). Despite the obvious substantive differences in these fields, they face a similar dilemma: the relevant literature establishes a relationship between an explanatory variable (X1) and some outcome (Y), controlling for other factors (X2), but researchers want to better understand how X1 generates Y. The question of how X1 generates Y is critical because sometimes a broader normative question turns on the nature of the processes linking X1 and Y (as in the case of the judicial behavior literature) or at other times a key policy issue depends on it (as in the case of the literature of SES and health outcomes, which seeks to identify mechanisms that can be manipulated in an effective and politically viable manner).

The resulting search for pathways often leads researchers into areas where they are uncertain about what mechanisms might be in play, whether and how they interact, and how they might be measured. In such situations, an increasingly common approach is to use mixed-method research that seeks to combine the existing quantitative large-N studies with process-tracing case studies. The instinct underlying mixed-method research is that quantitative and qualitative studies have complementary strengths. In the literature on judicial behavior, quantitative analysis of judicial voting allows a researcher to identify broad patterns across a large number of cases and to estimate the relationship between ideology and votes in specific cases, controlling for other factors. However, as every graduate student knows, "correlation is not causation," and for a variety of reasons social scientists have become increasingly skeptical of over-reliance on standard regression techniques applied to non-experimental, observational data (see, e.g., Achen 1986; Chatfield 1995; Freedman 1991; Kittel and Winner 2005; Winship and Sobel 2004; Gerber et al. 2004).

Case studies – intensive analyses of single units observed at a specific time or over a specific period of time, with the goal of offering insights into a population of cases (Gerring 2007) – promise a partial remedy to some these concerns. While it is difficult to eliminate the possibility of missing variables in explaining complex phenomena, case studies can often account for a wider range of factors than standard regression analyses, because they are not limited to the variables or measures of complex concepts that appear in preexisting datasets. By carefully plotting events and processes over time, case researchers can weave many observations from different levels of analysis into explanations, while gaining insights into the measure of the variables, their sequence, the direction of causality, and interactions among them. Case researchers are also not reliant on statistical tests of significance. They can triangulate among various types of data to gain confidence in their explanations as their findings converge on a single narrative. In addition, they can go back to the data as needed, consider the observable implications of alternative explanations that might arise as more is learned, and "stretch" their N by expanding the analysis over time or dividing cases into subunits to increase possible comparisons.

Given these strengths, case studies are a particularly promising means to explore the as-yet unobserved pathways between variables. Studying a small number of judicial decisions, for instance, would allow for the exploration of underlying decision-making processes by engaging in a detailed content analysis of a justice's reasoning of an opinion, how a justice uses existing precedents in that opinion, and whether the justice used the same precedents consistently over time. A case study could combine this type of content analysis with a review of justices' papers to search for clues about their motivations in deciding cases and with interviews of justices, law clerks, lawyers, and legal experts about the decision-making process. Questions might include: When did the justice indicate how she or he would vote on a case? Was it before oral arguments? Before reading the briefs? Was the justice interested in looking for a case to address this issue before the writ of certiorari was granted? Had the justice worked on similar cases before joining the Court? Which arguments seemed most persuasive to the justice: policy-oriented or rule-oriented ones? What is the justice's reputation among peers and the legal community? Is the justice known as a rule-oriented jurist or an "activist" one? While triangulating among diverse types of materials cannot reveal the "truth" about a justice's decision-making process – given our current technology, we cannot directly observe the ideological nature of the decision-making process as it unfolds inside a justice's brain – piecing together a number of causal process observations (CPOs) can get a researcher closer to understanding the underlying judicial decision-making process (Collier et al. 2004; Brady 2004; Bennett and George 2005). This can add valuable insight into the broader debate over the role of law versus ideology in Supreme Court decision-making (e.g., Gillman 1993, 2001).

Although case studies can be essential in tracing unmeasured processes linking variables, there is a trade-off of depth for breadth (Gerring 2004), making it difficult to assess the extent to which lessons learned from a single case (or a small number of cases) apply to the unobserved population of cases that feature the relationship of interest. Given this limitation, it is crucial to gain perspective on cases vis-à-vis the broader population. To do so, it seems wise to combine existing theoretical and empirical knowledge with information from quantitative literature to facilitate case selection and/or interpretation. In studying judicial decision-making, it would be useful if the existing quantitative data targeted cases where a justice's ideology seems to play different roles in different votes, and to assess how the key attributes of the cases selected compare to other cases within the broader population. As case studies accumulate, it is possible to begin to map the pathways between political ideology and votes, and to assess whether recent estimation techniques that seek to build knowledge on causal pathways can be used. This would improve confidence in the causal nature of the relationship and/or estimate the average effects of specific mechanisms.

This book is about how to do this. Specifically, it explains how to construct a pathway analysis: case studies aimed at (a) exploring the unobserved links in specific cases, and (b) using those insights to generate hypotheses about mechanisms in the unstudied population of cases featuring the X1/Y relationship. In addressing this topic, we explain how to prepare for pathway analysis by reading the relevant literature in light of different types of X1/Y relationships, how to select cases for pathway analysis, how to use the existing quantitative data to gain perspective on cases that have already been selected for practical or theoretical reasons, and how to use the results of pathway analysis to inform future studies of mechanisms. The central argument is that pathway analysis requires comparison and that researchers must choose cases in light of two criteria. The first is the *expected relationship between X1 and Y*, which is the degree to which cases are expected to feature the relationship of interest between X1 and Y in light of existing theory, empirical studies, and large-N data. The second is *variation in case characteristics*, or the extent to which the cases are likely to feature differences in criteria that can facilitate general knowledge. Our comparative approach stands in contrast to the standard advice in the field, which stresses the selection of single cases.

The book is intended for two audiences that share a considerable stake in the use of mixed-method research: quantitative scholars and qualitative scholars. We expect that it will be useful to quantitative scholars who want to use case studies to enrich their findings and assess whether they can take advantage of the latest estimation techniques that use mechanism knowledge to probe internal validity or to estimate the average marginal effects of specific mechanisms. Second, we expect that this work will be useful for qualitative scholars who want to use existing quantitative studies to select cases for exploring the unobserved links or processes between an explanatory variable and outcome. This group includes those who select cases at the initial stage of their research, as well as those who have completed an in-depth study of a single case (or small number of cases) and seek to gain perspective on the meaning of these cases or select additional cases for analysis.

1.2   Pathway analysis and the search for causal mechanisms

Political scientists, sociologists, and economists who agree on little else have embraced the search for causal mechanisms (Gerring 2010; Heckman and Smith 1995; Hedstrom and Ylikoski 2010; Imai et al. 2011; Mahlotra and Krosnick 2007; Mayntz 2004; Waldner 2007, 2012). A content analysis of top-ranked political science journals, many of which are predominantly quantitative, confirms the importance of mechanism-centered research in the discipline. In reviewing more than 1,400 articles published between 2005 and 2012, we found that more than 400 – about 30 percent – explicitly mentioned the importance of identifying mechanisms or causal processes.[2]

Pathway analysis offers a critical but imperfectly understood tool in the search for causal mechanisms, because it can provide a means to build a bridge from what is known about an association between variables to a better understanding of the unobserved links between variables and the feasibility of future mechanism-centered quantitative work. We believe that pathway analysis has not been utilized to its fullest potential in part because relatively little has been written about how researchers should select cases when the goal is to build knowledge of causal mechanisms that relates not just to the case at hand but also to unstudied cases, and in part because little has been written about how qualitative work relates to large-N studies of mechanisms. Moreover, what has been written does not address case selection when the underlying relationship between the explanatory variable and outcome is non-linear, there are

---

[2] Journals that were examined were: *Political Analysis, Annual Review of Political Science, American Journal of Political Science,* and *Comparative Political Studies.*

multiple causal pathways, or researchers desire to use an alternative to regression-based case selection.[3] As we will see in later chapters, under these circumstances, the existing guidelines may result in poor case selection that can produce false negatives, as it is possible to pick a case where the effect of the explanatory variable on the outcome is small and therefore hard to detect. This can lead researchers to miss important causal mechanisms or wrongly question the underlying relationship. Conversely, applying existing guidelines may produce false positives, as researchers may pick a case that involves a large, though atypical, effect or anomalous mechanism. Mistakes in the case selection process can imperil the research by leading to inaccurate conclusions and erroneous theoretical claims.

In this book we present a new approach for selecting cases for pathway analysis, which will help researchers effectively read the relevant literature on the underlying X1/Y relationship in preparation for their analysis; choose cases more systematically; better understand when and how to generalize from a single case or small number of cases to the unobserved population of cases; and assess the feasibility of future studies of mechanisms. An ancillary benefit of using our approach is improvement in both the transparency and reliability of the case selection process; this will facilitate assessment and aggregation of the findings of pathway analysis as mechanism-centered research agendas are pursued. Along the way, we will touch on broader issues such as the role of case studies in multi-method work and, equally important, how to assess their contributions in ways that fully acknowledge their importance while recognizing their inherent limits.

---

[3] The argument is *not* that scholars have failed to consider how to select cases for other types of research given causal complexity. There is a vast and useful literature on these topics (e.g., Brady and Collier 2004; George and Bennett 2005; Gerring 2007; King et al. 1994; Ragin 2000). The argument is that these issues remain undertheorized in the context of pathway analysis, which has very distinct analytic goals and thus requires distinct approaches to case selection.

1.3   Scope of the book

Before addressing our terminology and outlining the chapters that follow, a few points of clarification about the scope of our arguments are in order. First, our argument is not a philosophical inquiry into the nature of causal mechanisms (Elster 2007; Gerring 2010, 2008; Hedstrom 2005; Waldner 2012). Our approach is more pragmatic. We are interested in showing how to conduct pathway analysis, especially developing case selection techniques for researchers who want to use case studies to gain insights into how an explanatory variable (X1) generates an outcome (Y) and use those insights to generate hypotheses about the broader population of cases involving the X1/Y relationship. As discussed below, this analytic focus implies that causal mechanisms should be treated as unobserved links between two variables that are analogous to mediating or intervening variables in standard regression analyses (Imai et al. 2010; cf. Waldner 2012). Using this definition of mechanisms will enable qualitative researchers to take advantage of quantitative studies that establish associations among variables, as well as allow the case studies to be understood and used by quantitative researchers.

Second, our book does not address how researchers should *proceed* in the field, although we do address what types of questions ought to be *asked* in the field and, having already selected cases, how existing large-N data can be used to gain perspective on the cases. As such, our work is distinct from, yet also complementary to, the growing number of texts that describe process-tracing methods. In our view, it is telling that these works often analogize social science researchers to detectives trying to solve a particular crime (as opposed to investigating a pattern of criminal activity). Although this analogy may be useful for thinking about how researchers can reach causal inferences (the whodunit) from a small N, it can be misleading for our purposes. A hypothetical detective typically does not have to select which case to investigate, so there is no case *selection* problem. Equally important, a detective usually does not have to consider how findings from one investigation generalize to other crimes that have not been examined. In conducting pathway analysis, however, researchers have to make a choice about which cases to investigate and attempt to infer something about other, unobserved, unstudied cases that feature the relationship of interest. This detective analogy also implies that case studies will "solve" the crime. In pathway analysis, case studies help map mechanisms in a particular case and also serve as a bridge toward future studies, helping fill in the gaps between what is known and what needs to be known about mechanisms in a variety of settings. The knowledge gleaned from one crime case can stand alone. In research, knowledge from one case study is indispensable to the broader research agenda, but it must be kept in proper context given the state of the existing literature, the trade-offs associated with particular case selection strategies, and the need to test whatever hypotheses are drawn from the cases.

Third, our approach is distinct from other work on mixed-method research. It is true that, like others, we seek to help researchers make qualitative and quantitative studies work better together, so that they can take advantage of what are often complementary strengths and weaknesses of different types of studies. Yet our approach is far more explicit about embedding qualitative work in a broader mixed-method research agenda. Instead of encouraging researchers to use qualitative "soaking and poking" to probe the validity of existing quantitative findings, we urge researchers to read the existing literature in very particular ways, use quantitative data to select cases to map the underlying relationship of interest, and use the resulting map to assess the feasibility of meeting the analytic requisites of future quantitative studies. Indeed, one set of lessons of this book concerns the difficulties of using case studies to improve confidence in the causal nature of relationships. This is not a critique of case studies per se, but rather it is a recognition of the inherent difficulties of causal inference in a world of complex relationships.

Finally, this is a book about methods, not particular empirical findings. In evaluating examples of pathway analysis and case selection, our goal is to assess underlying research strategies, not to critique specific findings, as that would be inappropriate. In the context of pathway analysis, case selection does not guarantee accurate or valid findings; it does provide a rationale for selecting cases from a population and a basis for drawing inferences from a case to that population. We do, however, contrast our approach with specific examples from the literature and show how our approach suggests the selection of different cases.

1.4   Definitions and key terms

A discussion of terminology is unavoidable in this research area because many key concepts are contested and some have arguably been stretched to include multiple and sometimes incompatible meanings (for a list of important terms and their definitions, see the Glossary of terms). Accordingly, we need to define some key terms, beginning with the contested concept of "mechanism" (Elster 2007; Gerring 2010, 2008; Hedstrom 2005; Mayntz 2004; Norkus 2004; Waldner 2012). In a thoughtful review, John Gerring (2010: 1500–01) finds that the literature on mechanisms features many definitions, including the following:

(a) the pathway or process by which an effect is produced, (b) a micro-level (microfoundational) explanation for a causal phenomenon, (c) a difficult-to-observe causal factor, (d) an easy-to-observe causal factor, (e) a context dependent (tightly bounded or middle-range) explanation, (f) a universal (i.e., highly general) explanation, (g) an explanation that presumes probabilistic, and perhaps highly contingent, causal relations, (h) an explanation built on phenomena that exhibit law-like regularities, (i) a technique of analysis based on quantitative or case study evidence, and/or (j) a theory couched in formal mathematical models.

We have no desire to parse these conflicting definitions or make strong claims about which definition "best" captures the essence of the concept. Nevertheless, it is important to be clear about what we mean by this term and to locate our definition within the welter of interpretations in the literature. For starters, we agree that the meaning of mechanisms is highly context-specific, dependent on both the underlying type of research being conducted and the state of technology. A cognitive scientist might think of a mechanism differently than a political scientist, even though both may be interested in studying decision-making. Similarly, technological changes can make today's unobserved mechanisms into tomorrow's well-measured variables. For example, advances in brain imaging might allow us to directly view how justices think and distinguish between policy-oriented and law-oriented cognition.

Because we believe that the concept of mechanism depends on the nature and state of the relevant research agenda, it is important to relate our definition of mechanism to the nature of the type of research at the heart of the book: namely, pathway analysis. Pathway analysis has several inherent features that shape our definition of mechanism. First, pathway analysis, by its nature, explores the underlying links between some explanatory variable (X1) and some outcome (Y), controlling for other factors (X2). Accordingly, for purposes of pathway analysis, mechanisms are unobserved. (These unobserved factors may or may not be at a lower level of analysis than X1, X2, or Y.) This does not imply that mechanisms are *unobservable*, only that they are currently *unmeasured* in the large-N data.

Second, as we will see in a later chapter, the definition of pathway analysis implies that mechanisms lie between X1 and Y in a causal chain, and that variables in this chain can be seen as mechanisms for some research questions or as explanatory variables for other questions. Figure 1.1 illustrates this point as it presents two different research studies that both involve the same causal chain. In study 1 and study 2 (see Figure 1.1), X1 denotes the key explanatory variable of interest for *that* research study; the variables labeled X2 are variables other than the key explanatory variable for that study; and M1, M2, and M3 denote the mechanisms that connect X1 to Y. In study 1, the researcher is interested in the pathways that connect X1 to Y, and in particular the pathways

Study 1:

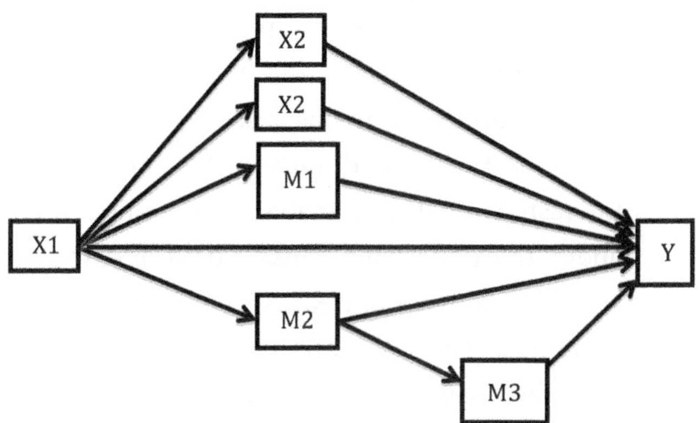

Note: X1 is the key explanatory variable; X2 are control variables; M1–M3 are unobserved mechanisms; and Y is the outcome.

Study 2:

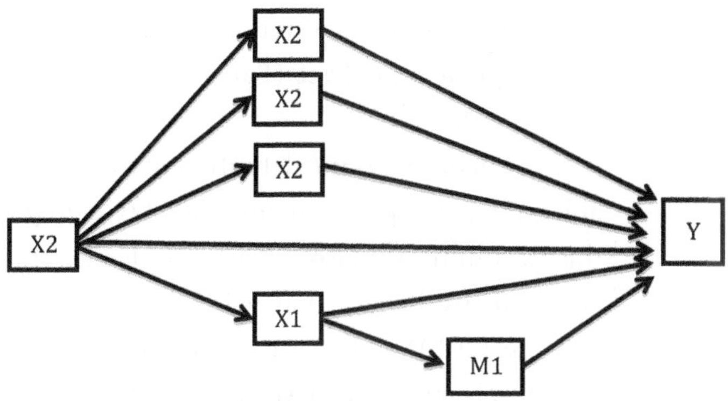

Note: X1 is the key explanatory variable; X2 are control variables; M1 is the unobserved mechanism; and Y is the outcome.

Figure 1.1   The contextual nature of mechanisms

represented by M1, M2, and M3. In this study, the X2 variables are measured and so they are not treated as mechanisms, even though they lie between X1 and Y in the causal chain.

Study 2 represents a scenario in which the researcher has decided to focus on a different part of the same causal chain. Now the key explanatory variable (X1) is in the middle of the causal chain and there is only one mechanism (M1) between the designated X1 variable and the outcome, Y. This example highlights that, even if the causal chain does not vary, how we conceptualize the various elements of the chain depends on the particular research question and state of knowledge in the field. As we will discuss in this book, a central task for researchers interested in pathway analysis is to embed their work in what is known about the underlying causal chain and to decide what to treat as a variable and what to treat as a mechanism.

Because pathway analysis is part of a mixed-method research agenda, it implies certain epistemological commitments. First, the mixed-method nature of pathway analysis means that quantitative and qualitative studies must share a common set of concepts, so any definition of mechanism must be compatible with the relevant estimation techniques. This means (as seen in Figure 1.1) mechanisms must be treated as conceptually analogous to mediating or intervening variables in standard regression analyses (Baron and Kenney 1986; Gerring 2012; Imai et al. 2010).

Second, our working definition of mechanisms implies that they can, at least in principle, be manipulated (Gerring 2012). We recognize that this assumption is also a matter of debate among philosophers of science, but we believe that it is reasonable. As a theoretical matter, as Gerring (2012) notes, claims about mechanisms imply that a mechanism's absence will have some effect on the underlying correlation between two variables. This suggests the ability, at least in theory, to remove or alter the mechanism; or, in other words, to manipulate it. As a substantive matter, this assumption is consistent with why at least some social scientists search for mechanisms. In seeking to develop policy prescriptions, for example, it may not be enough to know that there is a robust relationship between some explanatory variable (X1) and an outcome (Y), or even that they are causally related. Policy interventions may focus more on manipulating the mechanisms rather than the explanatory variable for which there may be an established association, because it is impossible to change some variables and politically infeasible to change others. Given these considerations, it would be odd to define mechanisms in a way that precluded manipulation. In sum, for our purposes of pathway analysis, mechanisms can be defined generally as unobserved factors that lie between an explanatory variable and an outcome in a causal chain. They are analogous to mediating or intervening variables that can, at least in theory, be manipulated.

Another definitional issue concerns our use of the term pathway analysis instead of the more familiar term process tracing, which is a method that "attempts to identify the intervening causal processes – the causal chain and causal mechanisms – between an independent variable (or variables) and the outcome of the dependent variable" (George and Bennett 2005: 206). Process tracing has been used in diverse types of research and in connection with a wide variety of claims, including research that seeks to describe how particular events emerge or that seeks to understand how causal mechanisms link variables throughout a population of cases (see generally, Bennett 2010; Collier 2011). Given its relevance in diverse types of research, it is thus potentially confusing to use it as a label to designate a distinct type of research.

For these reasons, although process-tracing techniques are obviously relevant in the search for causal mechanisms, we instead use the term pathway analysis to refer to research aimed at elucidating causal mechanisms underlying related variables in a population of cases (Gerring 2007). More specifically, pathway analysis is focused on understanding the connection(s) between a key explanatory variable and an outcome across different cases (as opposed to focusing on explaining a singular event or case). Although we are reluctant to add yet another term to the somewhat confusing lexicon of multi-method research, we believe that pathway analysis nicely captures the role of case studies in mixed-method, mechanism-centered research while avoiding some of the confusion that might arise by using the broader (but perhaps stretched) term process tracing.[4]

A final definitional issue concerns the meaning of equifinality in the context of pathway analysis. In general, equifinality means multiple causes of an outcome. For example, there are many possible ways a candidate can win an election, and the factors for success can combine in any number of patterns across a population of cases. In the context of pathway analysis, however, we are not interested in understanding how multiple factors $(X1, X2, \ldots Xj)$ can yield a result (Y). We are, rather, interested in how a particular $X1$ causes Y, controlling for other factors – that is, we want to know about the mechanisms that link $X1$ to Y. Under these circumstances, equifinality means the presence of multiple causal pathways between the specific variable $(X1)$ and outcome of interest (Y). As discussed in Chapters 6 and 7, Michael Ross (2004) argues that there are four mechanisms that connect natural resource wealth $(X1)$ with the onset of civil conflict (Y): looting, grievances among locals, incentives for separatism, and state weakness. Each of these different pathways is associated with the same explanatory variable, natural resource abundance, but natural resources can increase the likelihood of civil conflict through these four different mechanisms. This is what we mean by the "problem of equifinality."

1.5   Layout of the book

The remainder of our book is divided into three parts: (1) overview of method and its alternatives (Chapters 2, 3, and 4); (2) application of

---

[4] Note that our term of pathway analysis differs from Gerring's narrower concept of "pathway cases" (2007: 124–27). Pathway cases must feature the X1/Y relationship. As discussed throughout the book, pathway analysis often compares cases featuring varying expected relationships between X1 and Y to improve hypothesis generation in the face of uncertainty about how mechanisms function. As such, pathway analysis always encompasses pathway cases; it often includes other types of cases as well.

the case selection method (Chapters 5 and 6); and (3) contextualization of previously chosen cases (Chapters 7 and 8). Chapter 9 concludes the book.

Chapter 2 reviews how to prepare for pathway analysis by clarifying the distinct goals of pathway analysis, assessing whether its analytic requisites are met, and reviewing the literature in light of different types of X1/Y relationships and key measurement issues. Chapter 3 sets forth our case selection method in general terms, and Chapter 4 describes the main alternatives to our approach and compares the application of our method to its leading rivals using several textbook examples.

The section on case selection consists of two chapters, both of which apply our case selection methods using examples drawn from the substantive literature. Chapter 5 applies our method using the policy diffusion literature – studies on how policy choices spread across political boundaries – where researchers must decide how to frame the pathway analysis in light of a complex causal chain involving dynamic, temporal processes and non-linear models. Chapter 6 applies our method to the relationship between natural resources and civil conflict, and focuses on the use of matching as an alternative to regression-based case selection methods.

The section on contextualizing prior cases also consists of two chapters. Chapter 7 illustrates how researchers might use the tools developed in this book when they have already selected cases based on empirical, practical, or theoretical reasons but would like to use existing large-N data to gain perspective on these cases or to identify some cases for secondary analysis. Chapter 8 addresses how the results of pathway analysis can inform future studies of mechanisms, including future quantitative studies of mechanisms.

Chapter 9 brings the analysis full circle by reviewing how pathway analysis fits in the ongoing search for causal mechanisms. It argues that pathway analysis is a particularly promising bridge from what is now known about mechanisms to what is needed to understand them more fully. However, it cannot serve this purpose unless researchers have a better sense of the types of knowledge that need to be generated from case studies, how to select which cases to study, how to aggregate insights from cases as knowledge about mechanisms accumulates, and how to use these insights in considering future avenues of inquiry. Understanding the role of pathway analysis in the continuing search for mechanisms clarifies what constitutes good pathway analysis in a world in which knowledge about mechanisms is often limited and contested. We argue that it is critical to judge pathway analysis on its own terms, which involves mapping links between X1 and Y, as opposed to establishing internal validity or the average effects of specific mechanisms. Chapter 9 ends where we began, by considering why the search for mechanisms is a central part of the social sciences and will remain so for the foreseeable future.

Throughout the book, we use concrete examples and emphasize how our approach can help solve problems that arise under less-than-ideal conditions for pathway analysis, which often confront researchers in the field and often provide the rationale for doing case studies in the first place. Indeed, far from making the perfect the enemy of the good, our approach encourages researchers to see the current gap between what is known about causal mechanisms and what needs to be known to estimate them as an opportunity, one that seems particularly promising for researchers who want to use case studies in combination with quantitative analysis.

2 Preparing for pathway analysis

2.1 Introduction

The primary purpose of pathway analysis is to build knowledge about the causal mechanisms that link X1 to Y across settings. This implies the need to perform comparative analyses that can generate knowledge and/or hypotheses about the broader population of cases that feature the X1/Y relationship. Before delving into the details of case selection, it is important to consider how researchers should prepare for pathway analysis. As an initial matter, researchers must clarify their specific goals. Once oriented to the basic task, they should: (1) determine whether the basic analytic requisites of pathway analysis are met; (2) identify what is already known about the X1/Y relationship; and (3) take stock of relevant measures.

2.2 The threshold task: clarifying the goals of pathway analysis

The purpose of using pathway analysis differs from other, more familiar types of research, which is why it is important for researchers to clarify these goals from the start. On this score, James Mahoney and Gary Goertz (2006) usefully distinguish between two ideal types of research in the social sciences: causes of effects and effects of causes. Causes-of-effects research seeks to provide "thick description" of the emergence of singular events or outcomes in particular settings (Mahoney and Goertz 2006; see Brady and Collier 2004; Geertz 1973). For US politics or history research, for example, possible questions might include: Why

World War II? Why did the New Deal coalition collapse? What factors caused the most recent financial crisis? Why did the US Supreme Court decide *Bush* v. *Gore* as it did? For these types of questions, case selection is driven mostly by the substantive importance of the outcome to be explained, and the research primarily emphasizes case-specific internal validity ("Did the research get the story right?"), and not external validity ("Do the story's lessons apply in other contexts?"), although scholars often try to draw some broader lessons from their detailed descriptions.

Effects-of-causes research, by contrast, seeks to estimate the effect of a variable on an outcome across settings. So, instead of asking why a particular event occurred, these studies might ask: What is the relationship between regime type and war, or incumbency and reelection? Or what is the relationship between deregulation and financial crises, or political ideology and votes in Supreme Court decisions? Given these types of questions, case selection (or sampling) turns on the values of the key explanatory variables, controls, and outcomes (see, e.g., Geddes 1990; King et al. 1994). Because the research is intended to make causal inferences, its design needs to capture variation across the key explanatory variable and outcome and provide some basis for knowing how particular findings from among a few cases might apply to the unobserved population of cases. These strategies give rise to the standard rules of thumb regarding case selection, such as "don't select on the dependent variable."

Pathway analysis differs from both causes-of-effects and effects-of-causes research (see Table 2.1). Unlike studies that thickly describe particular cases, pathway analysis contributes to the understanding of the causal links between X1 and Y *across settings*, not just how an outcome emerges in a particular setting. Here, generalizability matters. This implies that it is not enough to target substantively important cases; in addition, a researcher must find ways to gain perspective on the cases selected and use the findings from these cases to generate hypotheses about the broader population of cases that feature the X1/Y relationship.

Table 2.1 Comparison of goals of causes of effects, effects of causes, and pathway research

Type of research	Goal
Causes-of-effects research	Provide thick description of how substantively important outcomes emerge in particular settings
Effects-of-causes research	Estimate average effects of X1 on Y
Pathway analysis	Understand how X1 causes Y in specific cases and generate hypotheses about mechanisms in the population of cases featuring the X1/Y relationship

Pathway analysis also differs from research that establishes the effect of X1 on Y. The main difference is that, in pathway analysis, the effect of X1 on Y is already established and thus the point is to better understand the substantive relationship implied by this finding – especially the links between X1 and Y – through the analysis of the X1/Y relationship in specific cases.[1] This implies that traditional guidelines for research design aimed at causal inference will likely be inappropriate. For example, the well-known admonition to avoid selecting cases on the dependent variable is irrelevant in the context of studying causal pathways because the very objective is to look for what connects an X1 variable to an outcome. Therefore a researcher will want to intentionally select cases using both what is known about the outcome and other factors to provide leverage over identifying the causal paths that connect X1 to Y.

The distinction between (a) the X1/Y relationship for purposes of pathway analysis and (b) an average treatment effect of X1 on Y or related measures of causal effects is absolutely critical. Pathway analysis ultimately seeks to understand substantive relationships *at the level of individual cases* and to use those insights to learn something about the population of cases that feature that substantive relationship. Average

---

[1] Researchers may use case studies to probe the validity of a contested relationship between X1 and Y; however, this is not the primary goal of pathway analysis.

treatment effects focus on *group-level differences* between treated and control and/or untreated units. So, in the case of US Supreme Court judicial behavior, the quantitative literature finds that, on average, judicial ideology significantly affects votes, controlling for other factors. In pathway analysis, we are interested in exploring the substantive relationship implied by this finding: the idea that liberal justices vote liberally and conservative justices vote conservatively. More specifically, researchers in this area would want to unpack *how* judicial ideology affects votes in specific cases *and* then hypothesize about how insights from the study of specific instances of judicial decision-making shed light on the population of Supreme Court decisions. As discussed in the next chapter, in selecting cases, researchers need a way to assess the values of X1, Y, the relevant controls, and expected relationship between X1 and Y for each individual unit in the population. This will allow researchers to select cases for comparative analysis, which can generate hypotheses about the links in the population of unstudied cases that feature the X1/Y relationship. Shifting from large-N studies that establish an average treatment effect to specific cases that feature the substantive X1/Y relationship is a central challenge of mixed-method research in general, and pathway analysis in particular. (As we will see, there is no guaranteed formula for this; instead, researchers need to use the tools at hand, recognize their limits, and be creative in searching for promising cases.)

2.3 Assessing analytic requisites

Given the goals of pathway analysis, the literature on the underlying X1/Y relationship must meet two minimal requirements. First, it must establish a robust relationship between X1 and Y that is likely to represent a causal relationship. We are well aware that confidence in whether an X1/Y relationship represents a causal effect will vary across settings. For purposes of analysis in the following chapters, we will assume that sufficient reasons exist to believe that the relationships in our examples are causal so that there is reason to investigate causal mechanisms. In practice, however, this assumption should not be made lightly.

Second, large-N datasets are needed that help understand (a) the functional form of the relationship between X1 and Y[2]; (b) the values of X1 and Y (and relevant controls) in specific cases; and/or (c) the expected magnitude and direction of the relationship between X1 and Y in individual cases. If the existing literature does not establish a robust relationship and provide useful data, then pathway analysis is not appropriate.

2.4   Assessing what is already known about the X1/Y relationship

It is axiomatic that researchers should review the relevant literature before embarking on any research, and pathway analysis is no exception. Pathway analysis is primarily directed at understanding an X1/Y relationship, so reviewing the literature to identify gaps in existing knowledge about that relationship and define the types of questions to be explored in the field is important. (In addition, as detailed in Chapter 8, understanding the structure of the X1/Y relationship in the terms set forth in this chapter will help to assess the feasibility of future quantitative studies using insights about mechanisms.)

The problem is that what is known about an X1/Y relationship can be obscured for a variety of reasons, including that relevant insights might be spread over a number of studies, which may or may not engage one another; researchers often bury assumptions about the relationship in their models; and they often do not use the same terms when describing

---

[2] Understanding the exact functional form is difficult. However, as we make clear, case selection requires that a researcher understand (or make assumptions about) the functional form of the X/Y relationship.

underlying processes or mechanisms. Under these circumstances, it is useful to develop some heuristics for organizing existing studies and identifying (and aggregating) their core findings as well as providing a tool to help reveal a researcher's own assumptions about the X1/Y relationship and how these assumptions might affect their research.

We believe that the key to this process is recognizing that there can be a variety of relationships among X1, Y, and the related mechanisms, and that these relationships imply distinct types of questions related to the case research and interpretation of the findings. One way to conceptualize these differences is to consider the four scenarios in Table 2.2, which represent paradigmatic examples of relationships between a key explanatory variable, the intervening mechanisms, and the outcome. In Table 2.2, X1 represents a key explanatory variable, M represents a mechanism, Y represents the outcome, and the arrows capture the direction of the relationship between these three. The scenarios are a simple way to present our understanding of the relevant relationships. If X1 is directly connected to Y, that captures a direct effect of X1 on Y. If X1 is connected to Y via a mechanism (M), then that is considered an indirect effect of X1 on Y. These scenarios describe the *overall* or aggregate pattern of relationships between X1, Y, and the Ms, and not whether the indirect, direct effects or both occur in a *specific* case. It is important to note that all of these scenarios are simplifications in that they feature only a very small number of mechanisms and the relationships are relatively straightforward. As noted in Chapter 1, and as discussed in later chapters, there are likely to be many more mechanisms and the relationships between them are likely to be quite complicated, but these simple scenarios encapsulate key analytic differences among distinct types of X1/Y relationships.

In the simplest case, scenario 1, the Single Pathway Scenario, the literature posits a single mechanism (M1) and a single pathway between X1 and Y, so that the entire X1/Y relationship occurs through the mechanism and the relationship between X1, Y, and M1 is either positive or negative. When there is only a single path and mechanism between X1

Table 2.2 Common scenarios for underlying relationships among causal variables, outcomes, and mechanisms

Scenario (description)	Graphical representation of the overall structure of the X1/Y relationship	Interpretation of graph
Scenario 1 (Single Pathway Scenario)	X1 ⟶ M1 ⟶ Y	There is only one mechanism X affects Y only through M1
Scenario 2 (Direct and Indirect Pathways Scenario)	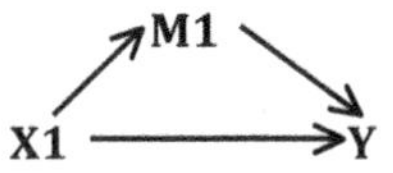 X1 → M1 → Y (direct and indirect pathways)	There is only one mechanism Mechanism represents one of the ways that X affects Y, but X may also directly affect Y regardless of M1
Scenario 3 (Multiple Exclusive Pathways Scenario)	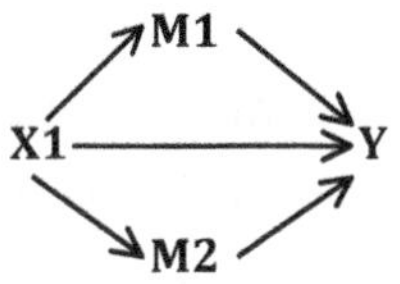 X1 → M1 → Y; X1 → M2 → Y	Mechanisms are mutually exclusive Mechanisms M1 and M2 represent possible ways that X affects Y, but X may also directly affect Y regardless of M1 and M2
Scenario 4 (Multiple Non-Exclusive Pathways Scenario)	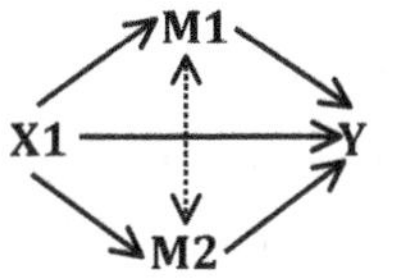 X1 → M1 → Y; X1 → M2 → Y; M1 ⤵ M2	Mechanisms can occur independently or simultaneously Observing M2 may be more likely if M1 is present than if M1 is absent, or vice versa The two mechanisms may interact to lead to a larger indirect effect on Y than the addition of each mechanism's indirect effect would suggest The mechanisms may cancel out each other's effects

and Y, the identification of a causal effect of X1 on Y implies the existence of the mechanism M1, because X1 can only affect Y via the M1 pathway. In this scenario, researchers might choose to focus their attention on two different issues. First, it may be useful to further unpack the relationship between X1 and Y by developing either a deeper understanding of how the X1 variable triggers the mechanism or how the mechanism affects the outcome (i.e., understanding how the arrows in the diagram function in practice). Second, it may be useful to know whether M1 functions similarly across all values of X1. Because this simple scenario seems unlikely for the complex phenomena studied by social scientists, it would also be useful to look for evidence that would immediately suggest that this is the inappropriate scenario, such as whether there are other variables that cause both X1 and Y, whether X1 has direct effects on Y, or whether there are other confounding variables that might cause both X1 and M1.

Scenario 2, the Direct and Indirect Pathways Scenario, is more complex. There is a single mechanism but more than one path between X1 and Y: a direct effect of X1 on Y and an indirect one caused by M1. This scenario is equivalent to partial mediation in which even after accounting for the mechanism/mediator, there is still a direct relationship between X1 and Y. If the causal relationship involves complete mediation, it means that that mechanism captures the entire effect of X1 on Y, and therefore the direct relationship is absent, which essentially reduces it to scenario 1, the Single Pathway Scenario.

Scenario 2 suggests a variety of related questions for pathway analysis. For example: Does the direct effect of X1 on M1 only exist for certain values of X1? Where M1 is present, is the relationship with the outcome entirely mediated by M1 (as in scenario 1)? If this is possible, then a reasonable purpose of pathway analysis is to shed light on what values of X1 are associated with the direct and/or indirect effect. Researchers must be careful as to how any single case under this scenario is interpreted. Unlike the Single Pathway Scenario, the failure to observe M1 in scenario 2 does not necessarily raise questions about the X1/Y relationship as posited, because X1 can directly affect Y even without M1. Moreover, even if M1 is observed in a single case, that case cannot offer an answer as to whether that mechanism functions similarly across values of X1 or whether particular case characteristics are associated with the presence or absence of M1, both of which are important questions for understanding how M1 links X1 and Y. In addition, it is important to try to understand whether M1 occurs without X1, and whether M1 co-varies with other Xs. This information is useful in trying to understand more fully the ways that the key explanatory variable affects an outcome.

Scenario 3, the Multiple Exclusive Pathways Scenario, features multiple mechanisms and paths (so that there are direct and indirect effects), and the mechanisms are mutually exclusive. In general, case studies in research settings such as this one should focus on developing a better understanding of the mechanisms. Why are the mechanisms mutually exclusive? If one occurs does it block the other from occurring? Or, are certain values of X1 associated with M1 rather than M2? Are both mechanisms positively associated with the outcome or do the mechanisms differ in their relationship with the outcome? Answering all of these questions would be useful in fully understanding the X1/Y relationship.

Scenario 4, the Multiple Non-Exclusive Pathways Scenario, presents the most complicated situation: multiple pathways and multiple, possibly interactive mechanisms, which add the possibility that M1 and M2 are related. In pursuing case studies, researchers must ask: Are the mechanisms related? Under what conditions does one, the other, or both occur? Do values of X1 associate with any pattern of the mechanisms? The number of possible interactions between X1 and M1 and M2 in this scenario constrains the general conclusions reached from case studies, because it is difficult to tell if a given case is typical of all of the possible relationships. In this situation, researchers would want to eventually understand all of the various relationships in the diagram, which is a huge challenge but it also presents tremendous opportunities for case studies to add to the substantive understanding of the X1/Y relationship.

To this point, we have assumed that the literature allows a researcher to determine whether an X1/Y relationship resembles one of the scenarios in Table 2.2. However, what is known about the causal mechanisms will often be quite limited, thus researchers will simply not know which scenario best captures the underlying relationship. There are, for example, many studies that establish robust positive or negative relationships but provide limited insight into the possible mechanisms underlying them. In these cases, the association among variables is largely a "black box" and the underlying relationship might fall under any of the four scenarios. In myriad academic areas, some relevant literature may suggest that multiple pathways link a variable and an outcome but fail to fully specify the paths. Other studies may specify multiple likely mechanisms but do not address how they function across different case characteristics, how they might interact with each other, or how they relate to other variables. Under either of these conditions, a researcher can have confidence that neither scenario 1 nor scenario 2 applies (because there are multiple mechanisms), but cannot be sure whether the relationship more closely resembles scenario 3 or scenario 4 (because there is uncertainty about the relationships between the multiple mechanisms).

If there is a basic lack of knowledge about the structure of the relationship between X1, Y, and M(s), then the primary task of pathway analysis is hypothesis generation about which scenario best captures the underlying relationship. To do this, it is necessary to adopt a comparative research strategy, and the comparative case studies will mainly be useful for probing four issues: (1) the number of likely mechanisms underlying the X1/Y relationship (or the lower bound estimate of them); (2) the relationships among different mechanisms, including whether they interact and their potential observational equivalence; (3) the extent to which mechanisms (and how they function) are related to values of other key explanatory variables and possible confounds; and/or (4) the observable implications or measures of mechanisms.[3]

To see how the scenarios in Table 2.2 might be useful in reviewing literature in preparation for pathway analysis, consider the example involving judicial ideology and US Supreme Court decisions. In reading this literature, there are a large number of quantitative studies

---

[3] Kosuke Imai and colleagues (2013) present a similar list of goals for building knowledge about causal mechanisms, but present no guidelines for how such knowledge should be developed. They suggest scholars should: identify the other possible causal mechanisms, identify ways to measure these other mechanisms, and theorize about and gain knowledge about how the multiple mechanisms interact with each other, if they interact at all.

that establish an association between ideology (X1) and justices' votes (Y). By itself, however, this empirical regularity is silent on the links connecting X1 and Y; the association is a black box; the mechanisms are unmeasured. If the literature stopped at this point, we would not know which scenario best captured the relationship and thus would ask questions relating to the basic structure of the X1/Y relationship, such as: Are there both direct and indirect effects of ideology on votes? How many modes of decision-making underlie this relationship? If multiple, are they mutually exclusive or do they interact? How do these processes relate to other Xs, such as the identity of the litigants or policy area of the decision?

In the judicial behavior literature there is a debate between the behavioralists and postbehavioralists on the role of ideology in US Supreme Court decision-making. Although not framed in terms of underlying mechanisms, we interpreted this debate as positing two underlying, unobserved processes that potentially connect judicial ideology and votes: instrumental judging and good faith judging, which seem mutually exclusive as they posit distinct roles for ideology in the decision-making process. Moreover, there are detailed case studies, such as Howard Gillman's (2001) analysis of the *Bush* v. *Gore* litigation, which argue that examples of purely instrumental, partisan judging occur, but are relatively rare. Taken together, this literature suggests that scenario 3 applies: there are multiple, mutually exclusive links between ideology and votes. Given this reading of the literature, the focus of pathway analysis is not on probing the basic structure of the X1/Y relationship; rather the focus should be on using comparative case studies to explore the conditions under which each type of judging emerges.

The broader point here is that the scenarios in Table 2.2 can help researchers analyze the relevant literature about the underlying X1/Y relationship in preparation for pathway analysis and help point them toward concrete questions that are crucial for understanding the substantive relationship of interest. Knowing the type of knowledge to be

Table 2.3 Examining measurement validity of large-*N* indicators

		Quantitative evidence	
		Variable (or mechanism) absent	Variable (or mechanism) present
Qualitative evidence	Variable (or mechanism) present	Invalid measure	Valid measure
	Variable (or mechanism) absent	Valid measure	Invalid measure

developed is useful before engaging in detailed qualitative work and comparing the findings of specific cases.

2.5   Taking stock of measurement issues

Although not the main focus of this book, measurement is always a concern in multi-method research, and it is useful to assess the literature in light of two types of measurement issues in pathway analysis. First, as discussed in Chapter 1, we define mechanisms as unobserved links between X1 and Y. As such, one of the goals of case study research is to build measures of mechanisms (either direct measures or proxies) from the ground up by identifying observable implications of different mechanisms. These observable implications, in turn, can provide the basis to develop measures for future large-N studies or secondary case studies aimed at gaining perspective on cases already selected for theoretical or practical reasons.

Second, to the extent that a relevant literature offers measures of the key variables, case studies can be used to probe the validity of these measures. As seen in Table 2.3, it is possible for researchers to compare measures in large-N studies in the literature with the findings in their case studies so as to probe whether in fact the large-N measures serve as reliable proxies for the appearance of the variable in their cases. If large-N measures and case study findings match, this improves confidence in the measure; if not, it is necessary to question the validity of the measure. Note that if a case study casts doubt on the validity of the measures of X1 or Y variables, a researcher may need to rethink whether there is a reliable relationship between X1 and Y – and hence whether pathway analysis is appropriate at all.

2.6 Conclusion

This chapter reviews how to prepare for pathway analysis and underscores some key issues that recur throughout the book. First, pathway analysis is a distinct mode of inquiry, which implies characteristic strategies for reading the relevant literature and for selecting cases (which we elaborate on in the next chapter). Accordingly, after clarifying the goals of pathway analysis, it is crucial to read the literature to determine whether the state of knowledge meets the analytic requisites for pathway analysis, what is already known about the X1/Y relationship, and the state of knowledge about the measurement of mechanisms, key variables, and outcomes.

Second, in most situations, there will be considerable gaps in knowledge about the mechanisms that connect X1 to Y, so the primary goal for pathway analysis is to gain knowledge about how a key explanatory variable is related to the outcome. The scenarios listed in Table 2.2 can help researchers wade through and organize the relevant literature on the X1/Y relationship, identify its gaps, frame the questions driving their case studies, and reveal their own assumptions about the links connecting X1 and Y. Of course, these scenarios are not meant to paint researchers into a box regarding what relationships are possible in a given empirical example, but they can provide useful touchstones when preparing for pathway analysis.

Third, when confronted with uncertainty about the structure of the X1/Y relationship researchers should adopt a comparative research strategy and use the cases to explore which scenario seems to best capture the relationship. To do so, they should focus on four key issues: (1) the number of mechanisms linking X1 and Y; (2) the relationships among different mechanisms; (3) the extent to which mechanisms – and how they function – are related to the values of other key explanatory variables and possible confounds; and/or (4) measurement of mechanisms, the key variables, and outcomes. Having completed these preliminary tasks, researchers will be ready to select cases for pathway analysis, which is the subject of the next chapter.

3 Case selection for pathway analysis

3.1 Introduction

Researchers have long recognized that "the cases you choose affect the answers you get" (Geddes 1990). Accordingly, it is critical to select cases carefully and in a transparent manner. This chapter lays out our general approach for selecting cases for pathway analysis. It begins by briefly reviewing the analytic goals of pathway analysis and how they relate to the general criteria for case selection. It then outlines some of the key challenges in applying these criteria and ends with practical advice for implementing these general principles.

3.2 The goals of pathway analysis and case selection

As discussed in the last chapter, pathway analysis ultimately has two goals: (1) to gain insight into the mechanisms that connect some explanatory variable (X1) and some outcome (Y) in specific cases; and (2) to use the insights from these cases to generate hypotheses about mechanisms in the unstudied population of cases that feature the X1/Y relationship.

These two goals, in turn, imply several principles for case selection (see Figure 3.1). The first goal of pathway analysis suggests the *expected relationship* criteria, which means the degree to which individual cases

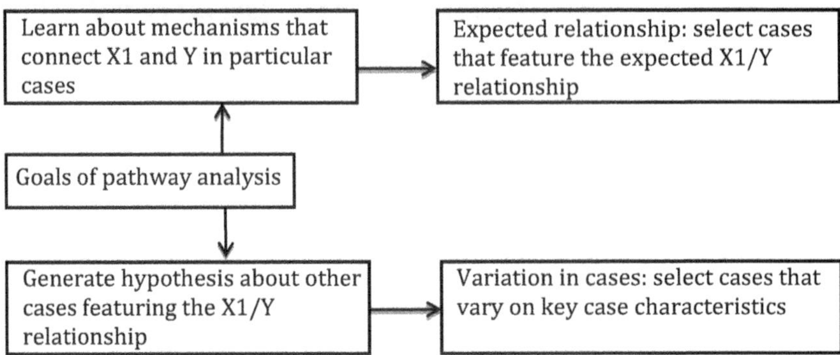

Figure 3.1   Goals of pathway analysis and criteria for case selection

are expected to feature the relationship of interest between X1 and Y given existing theory, empirical knowledge, and large-N studies. It is perhaps obvious, but studying mechanisms that underlie the X1/Y relationship requires identifying cases where the X1 variable is related to the Y, controlling for possible confounds (X2) (Gerring 2007). If the relationship between X1 and Y differs based on the values of X1, then a researcher needs to understand how the relationship depends on the value of X1.

The second goal of pathway analysis implies the need to consider *variation in case characteristics*, meaning the extent to which the cases selected vary in terms of the X1/Y relationship, the X values, and the Y values. If it is not known how X1 generates Y, comparing cases that feature different values of X1, likely "levels" of the X1/Y relationship, and outcomes may help gain perspective on the findings and generate hypotheses.

3.3   Expected versus observed X1/Y relationships

Readers will note that choosing cases based on the expected X1/Y relationship does not guarantee that the selected cases will, in fact, feature the X1/Y relationship – *expected* relationships are not the same as *observed* relationships. Even if researchers have strong theoretical or empirical reasons to believe that specific cases will feature particular X1/Y relationships or believe they know how the large-N data relate to the presence of mechanisms in specific cases, there is no guarantee that these expectations will be met. Theories or empirical knowledge could be wrong, there might be some mechanisms that block the X1/Y relationship, or researchers might just be unlucky and happen to pick anomalous cases.

The need to select cases using observed characteristics when the actual interest is in yet-unobserved characteristics (that is, causal mechanisms) is a key problem for researchers interested in using mixed methods to study causal mechanisms. Although we argue it is useful to use large-N data to guide case selection, the use of quantitative data to understand the expected X1/Y relationships at the level of individual cases does not eliminate the possibility that a researcher's expectations will fail to match up to actuality. This raises the question of how best to use large-N data to select individual cases.

There is no foolproof means to do this. All things being equal, we argue it is useful to select cases using what is known about the values of the explanatory variable (X1), the controls (X2), the outcome (Y), *and* the best estimates of the expected relationship between the X1 and Y variables. So, for example, suppose researchers run an experiment on getting out the vote and find that a phone call from a neighbor 24 hours before an election has a significant effect on turnout. They then might want to understand *how* the phone call affects turnout; that is, what are the unobserved mechanisms that connect the call to turnout? Is it the tone of the call or the caller's voice? The timing of the call? The specific content of the conversation? The degree to which a caller has a personal connection to the voter? Or some combination of these factors or other ones?

To begin to understand the possible mechanisms that connect the phone call to an increase in average turnout, we might want to conduct interviews or focus groups with registered voters in the study. In the absence of good theoretical or empirical reasons to guide the selection of specific voters, it seems reasonable to use the existing data on voter turnout to look for interesting comparisons. Specifically, we can use the existing data from the voting experiment to identify registered voters who (a) we know received the call ($X1 = 1$), (b) we expect that the phone call increased the probability of voting, and (c) nonetheless differ in the outcome ($Y = 0$ in one case and $Y = 1$ in the other). After we identify individuals who we believe meet these three criteria, we could then use surveys and/or interviews to investigate the mechanisms that led to the decision to vote and whether the mechanisms differed between voters. Instead, we might select registered voters who received the treatment and voted, but who differed in their predicted probability of voting, because such a comparison may provide insight into whether the mechanisms varied across types of voters. Alternatively, we might use matching techniques to find registered voters who are most similar to each other based on observables (i.e., on $X1$ and the controls, $X2$) but differ in the outcome. Neither strategy guarantees that the researchers would discover all of the mechanisms underlying the $X1/Y$ relationship or that they could discover "typical" mechanisms, but comparing voters in this manner would be a promising place to start exploring how $X1$ causes Y and building theory about the structure of the $X1/Y$ relationship.

Researchers need to understand the potential gap between the expected $X1/Y$ relationship and the observed $X1/Y$ relationship (regardless of whether knowledge of the expected relationship comes from existing theory, large-N estimates, or substantive knowledge). This is one reason why we urge scholars to adopt a comparative approach: selecting multiple cases based on the available information – theoretical, substantive, large-N data – serves as a hedge against the possibility that some of the cases selected might fail to feature the $X1/Y$ relationship as expected. However, even cases in which prior expectations about the $X1/Y$ relationship are not met can be useful, provided that a researcher asks the right types of questions in the case study. Specifically, if a researcher finds gaps between the expected and observed X1/Y relationship, the questions to ask include: Why did the prediction about the X1/Y relationship fail? Was there a mechanism that blocked the expected effect of X1 on Y? Does the case simply fail to feature the X1/Y relationship? If so, what does this failure suggest about the understanding of the X1/Y relationship or the relevant measures? Is the case an anomaly or does it require rethinking the association between X1 and Y? Tracing the emergence of X1 over time within the case study would be particularly useful in considering these questions, all of which are relevant to the search for mechanisms and the quest to better understand the X1/Y relationship.

3.4 Practical steps for implementing expected relationships and case variation criteria

Assessing the trade-offs between expected relationships and variation in case characteristics can be difficult. If it is known that there is only one mechanism linking X1 and Y, and that it functions consistently across both the values of X1 and the expected X1/Y relationship, then it is not necessary to be concerned with variations in case level attributes. More commonly, however, a researcher will not know the number of mechanisms, how they interact, or whether they function consistently. Given this uncertainty, it is important to select more than one case for pathway analysis, and these cases should vary across a variety of relevant dimensions, so a set of cases *taken together* provide opportunities for comparisons that offer some leverage on both criteria. While there is no mechanical formula for applying these criteria, the following steps are useful.

3.4.1 Visualizing variation in the data

To zero in on promising cases for analysis, we suggest that researchers create a visualization of the available information. The specific form of this visualization will depend on the context, the nature of the data, and the underlying models in the relevant literature. As a practical matter, it will often be useful to begin by examining the X1 values in a histogram (or other distributional plot) to understand the distribution of this variable. This information will help inform how a researcher thinks about both the expected relationship and case variations, especially where the knowledge of causal mechanisms is limited.

Once there is a sense of the distribution of the X1 variable, the next step will typically be to assess the expected relationship for each case. This differs from trying to identify the average treatment effect of the X1 variable, because rather than identifying the average relationship across the cases we want to estimate the *expected* X1/Y relationship for a given case in the dataset. There are a variety of approaches to how researchers might assess the expected relationship, in addition to using existing theory and empirical studies, which might be scant. We now present brief discussions of different approaches. The goal is to begin building a tool kit that can be used to tackle specific substantive examples, not to provide an exhaustive list of possibilities.

One way to assess the expected relationship is to compare the residuals or predicted probabilities from a model that includes X1 to the residuals/predicted probabilities from a model that excludes X1.[1] In either case, the expected relationship is highest for cases where the inclusion of X1 is associated with a large difference in the predictions from the regression. Under this approach, the expected relationship is the estimate of the total relationship between X1 and Y, which includes the direct effect of X1 and the indirect effect of the M. It is important to remember that this is *not* sampling on or estimating an unobserved mechanism; instead, it is using the data to help locate cases that feature the expected

---

[1] Where Y is a continuous variable, it is possible to compare residuals between regression models that include and exclude X1; where Y is not continuous, it is possible to compare the predicted probability of a given outcome for each observation with and without X1.

X1/Y relationship, which will be unpacked in the qualitative analysis of the case.

Another way to assess the expected relationship is to estimate the relationship between X1 and Y value at multiple values of X1.[2] This information can then be used to select cases in which the value of X1 is associated with a large estimated change in Y. This approach, which we call the marginal effect approach, focuses on the expected relationship at different values of X1 rather than on the expected relationship for specific observations/cases. This approach can be used to examine how the expected relationship between X1 and Y changes when we modify the value of one of the other variables (X2) in the statistical model. For instance, in studying war, a researcher might have reason to believe that the mechanisms that link natural resources (the X1) to civil conflict (Y) depend upon a country's level of democracy (X2).[3] In such a case, a researcher needs to examine the estimated relationship between natural resources and conflict at different levels of democracy. This information can be used to select cases for probing how a mechanism might depend on the level of democracy. In general, the marginal effect approach is most useful when researchers want to investigate particular values of X1 or X2 and need a way to estimate the expected relationship given these values. This approach can also aid in identifying the expected relationship for cases where there are some missing data, which precludes comparing residuals or predicted probabilities.

An alternative tool to estimate the expected relationship is to utilize a form of matching to identify comparable cases. Matching is a useful alternative for two primary reasons: (1) it allows a researcher to relax the functional form assumptions of regression-based case selection, and

---

[2] This could be a useful strategy even for linear models like OLS, if the estimated model contains higher-order terms or interactions between variables.

[3] This is a more complicated scenario because in this scenario another variable, X2, works in conjunction with X1 to determine which mechanisms are present.

(2) it is explicitly designed to identify comparisons between cases, although usually comparisons between groups of cases rather than between individual cases. There are many different ways to implement matching, so we first discuss a basic approach, and then apply this method in a later chapter.

Consider a situation in which there is a dichotomous outcome (Y), a continuous key explanatory variable (X1), and a vector of other variables (X2). Using the X2 variables it is possible to compute the Mahalanobis distance (Stuart and Rubin 2007) between every two observations, which provides a measure of similarity based on the vector of X2 variables for each pair of observations.[4] It is also possible to compute the distance between each pair of observations on the key explanatory (X1) variable. This means that for each potential pair of cases, a researcher would now have a measure of similarity on X1 and X2, and would also know whether the two cases have different or similar outcomes (Y). From this information, a researcher can thus choose a variety of different cases to compare. For instance, from the perspective of the expected relationship, one choice might be to use the distance measure calculated from the X2 variables to identify (for each outcome case) the closest non-outcome case. This would create a most similar match (across the vector of X2 variables) between each outcome and non-outcome case. From the various matched pairs of cases (all of which differ on the outcome) a researcher could choose matched pairs that are maximally distant in the

---

[4] Although many matching approaches utilize the propensity score method, we do not use that method here. The reason is that the approach we outline is similar to a case control study in which the outcome is known in advance and there is an attempt to understand why and how that outcome occurred, but a researcher is not estimating the propensity to receive treatment. In addition, the Mahalanobis distance can be computed for any pair of cases, allowing for the identification of cases that are most similar or different on the key explanatory variable (X1), the observed matching variables (the vector of X2), or the outcome (Y). In essence this approach provides researchers with important flexibility. Even if the Mahalanobis distance is inferior to the propensity score distance for causal inference, its flexibility makes it superior for pathway analysis (Gu and Rosenbaum 1993; Rubin and Thomas 2000).

value of the key explanatory variable but similar on their X2 values. This is one way to target cases with a large expected relationship because the matched variables are similar while the values of X1 and Y differ. If the outcome differs between the two cases, but they are otherwise similar in multidimensional space, this is one way to have a large expected relationship between the X1 and Y. There are other ways to use this information to guide case selection, and we explore those alternatives in Chapter 6. In general, how we utilize matching techniques to select cases will depend on the goals of a particular set of comparisons and no one set of guidelines will be applicable for all research questions.

These preceding steps, along with existing large-N data, offer several pieces of information for locating interesting patterns of variation in case characteristics. The challenge becomes how to organize these bits of information into a useful format. Again, there is no mechanical way of doing this, but one effective strategy, which we describe in later chapters when we discuss implementing pathway analysis, is to make a scatterplot where the X-axis includes the X1 values, the Y-axis is a score reflecting the expected X1/Y relationship in a given case (how these measures are generated will be discussed in later chapters), and each point on the scatterplot can be labeled with the observed Y-value and case name.

We will elaborate on this step when we turn to specific applications of our method, but we can foreshadow some important principles with a simple hypothetical, which assumes a regression-based approach to case selection. Figure 3.2 illustrates a scatterplot that allows us to visualize the expected relationship and variation in case characteristics (we will return to similar plots in later chapters). This example assumes there is a positive relationship between X1 and Y, and that Y is a dichotomous variable. The Xs on the graph represent cases where an outcome occurs (Y = 1); the solid circles represent cases where an outcome did not occur (Y = 0).

We assume that we know very little about the mechanisms that connect X1 and Y, and thus cannot identify which scenario from Table 2.2 represents this situation, which is one of the important goals of pathway

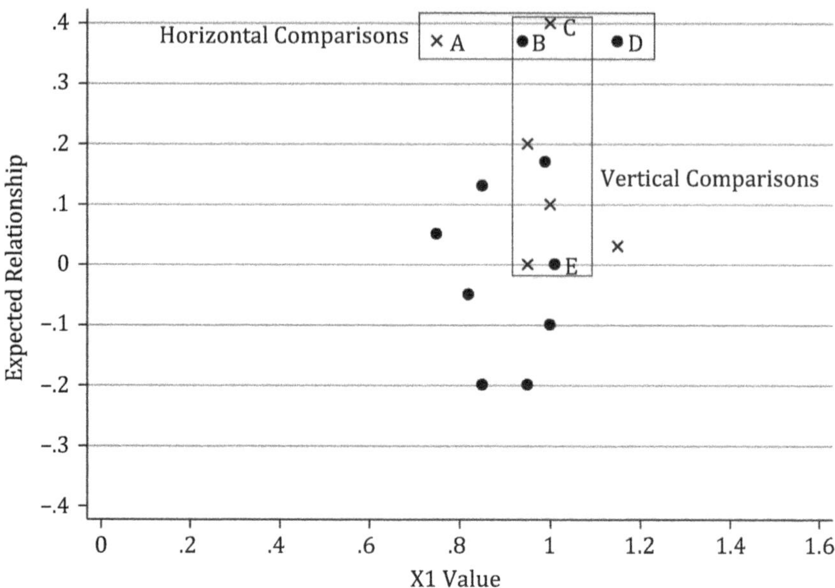

Note: ● = non-outcome   × = outcome

Figure 3.2   Scatterplot with expected relationship, X1 value, and observed outcome

analysis. It is also worth reminding readers that to shed light on the pathways between X1 and Y, it is crucial to select multiple cases for comparison, because to gain knowledge about whether a mechanism connects the X1 variable to the outcome requires, at the very least, an understanding of how the mechanism is either present or absent across a variety of cases. To put it another way, observing a mechanism in a single case does not tell a researcher whether that mechanism is actually related to the X1/Y relationship unless there is a well-developed theory about the relationship of X1, Y, and M(s).

In working with this scatterplot, it is useful to think both vertically and horizontally in order to identify potentially interesting variations among the X1 values, relationships between X1 and Y, and Y outcomes. By thinking vertically, we mean looking for cases with similar X1 values, which can include comparisons of cases with different levels of expected relationships or different Y outcomes. By thinking horizontally, we mean looking for cases with different values of X1 but similar levels of the expected relationships and/or Y outcomes.

Thinking vertically, a researcher might choose to compare, for example, cases B and C in Figure 3.2, because the two cases feature similar X1 values and expected relationships between X1 and Y, but the outcomes differ. The first question to ask is whether different mechanisms are present in the two cases. Perhaps case B lacks the mechanisms that might link X1 to Y, which would help to explain how X1 is associated with a mechanism. Other information to determine might be whether case C features a mechanism that B lacks, or if there was a second mechanism in case B that blocks the effect of the other mechanism.

Another potentially useful vertical comparison could be cases C and E. In case C, it is expected that X1 has a large effect on Y and, in fact, the outcome occurs. In case E, it has a similar X1 value, but Y does *not* occur. That raises some interesting questions. Does case C have a mechanism that case E does not (consistent with scenario 1, the Single Pathway Scenario, that posits no direct effect between X1 and Y)? Do both cases C and E share some common mechanisms, but E features an additional mechanism that blocks the outcome from occurring (consistent with scenario 4, where multiple mechanisms interact)? Such a comparison can help to demonstrate why a single case may not be helpful, because if only case C were studied, a researcher might believe that the identified mechanism is sufficient to connect the cause to the outcome; however, case E would help to understand that the mechanism from case C is not necessarily associated with the outcome. Alternatively, if only case E were studied, it might not be understood that an observed mechanism could be associated with the outcome if there are no other mechanisms present to block its effect.

In comparing horizontally, a researcher could select cases A and C, each of which features a similar expected relationship and outcome, but the X1 values vary. Here, we suggest focusing on whether the same mechanisms that link X1 and Y work across the X1 values (consistent with scenario 1, the Single Pathway Scenario). Does X1 directly affect Y in either of these cases (consistent with scenario 2, the Direct and Indirect Pathways Scenario)? Or are there multiple mechanisms (consistent with scenarios 3 and 4, the Multiple Exclusive and Multiple Non-Exclusive Pathways Scenarios)? We also suggest exploring the similarities between cases A and C. Do both of these cases feature some mechanism that is absent in cases B and D (consistent with scenario 1, the Single Pathway Scenario)? Is there some mechanism that blocks the outcome in cases B and D that is absent in cases A and C (consistent with scenario 4, the Multiple Non-Exclusive Pathways Scenario)?

In selecting cases, the goal is to keep in mind the state of the existing literature and the ultimate goals of the multi-method research agenda. Specifically, we want to stress that using comparisons can help gain a better sense of the underlying structure of the X1/Y relationship, which includes: the number of mechanisms connecting X1 and Y; understanding the relationship among multiple mechanisms (including whether all mechanisms are positive or negative, and whether some mechanisms cancel each other out); whether the mechanism(s) occurs in the absence of expected effects or outcomes; the possibility of observing the key explanatory variable without a mechanism appearing; and the relationship between mechanisms that link X1 and Y and other explanatory variables.

3.4.2   Case control strategies

There are a very limited number of cases in Figure 3.2. However, in an actual example, the data used to establish the X1/Y relationship will be far more extensive, so that thinking vertically and horizontally might yield many possible comparisons. Faced with a large number of potentially promising cases and limited resources, researchers should seek ways to exercise case control to maximize the analytic leverage of their cases. In case control research designs used in epidemiology or medicine, one selects subjects who contracted a disease and subjects who did not have the disease, and then studies subject behavior and backgrounds prior to contracting the disease to see if those with the disease differ systematically from those without the disease in a way that we suspect would be related to contracting the disease. This is a very weak research design for causal inference, but it can help to generate hypotheses about the differences between the two groups that would warrant investigation via another research design. The same basic approach can be used for pathway analysis. In the basic approach, researchers would often want to select cases that differ in the outcome and the value of the key explanatory variable, but that appear to be similar on the other dimensions (i.e., the predicted probability or outcome from a regression, the multivariate distance in a matching approach, or perhaps a single attribute such as geographic region or time period). More generally, the idea of case control means that researchers intentionally choose cases that are similar on known dimensions but that differ in ways that allow generation of knowledge about a particular research question. Again, there is no cut-and-dried rule for how to do this, but throughout this book we provide guidance about common strategies of case control. This type of purposive sampling, which we discuss in later chapters, can determine how to prioritize specific cases to use for pathway analysis.

3.5 A note on random sampling strategies

One might be tempted to use stratified random sampling instead of our purposive approach. In the sampling approach, researchers identify cases that have similar X1 values and then randomly select a case or cases from within each group of X1 values (one could select based on something other than X1 values, too). The idea is that within each stratum of X1 values a researcher could, via random selection, choose cases that differ in their expected relationship despite having similar X1 values. Stratified random sampling reduces the opportunities to intentionally choose cases that support a researcher's favored theory. While there are useful applications for stratified random sampling, there are also serious limitations. One is that, given the small number of cases likely to be sampled, it will still not be possible to make generalizations with the precision usually accorded to random sampling. A wider limitation is that any random sampling approach will not allow the use of case control strategies, because within a given stratum the cases are selected at random rather than purposively. The key to our case control approach is to select cases that are similar in an important aspect (such as the expected X1/Y relationship), but that also differ in an important dimension (often the outcome). Picking cases randomly from multiple homogeneous regions of the X1 value, as in stratified random sampling, cannot ensure that the cases selected are similar in other important ways. For instance, it may be useful to purposively select cases from similar geographic regions or from a similar time period in a panel dataset, to ensure that any unmeasured attributes can be accounted for. Therefore, while the stratified random sampling approach can be useful, we believe that the additional aspects of control allowed in fully purposive case selection will most often benefit any research, and thus we use fully purposive case selection throughout the book. However, we are also aware that random sampling has value in pathway research, and so we also discuss instances in which it may be preferable to a purposive strategy.

3.6   Summary

Figure 3.3 draws key material from both Chapters 2 and 3 to provide a schematic overview of the practical steps of our approach. After clarifying the goals of pathway analysis, researchers should: (1) assess whether the analytic requisites for pathway analysis are met (i.e., there is a robust relationship between X1/Y and available data); (2) review the relevant literature on the X1/Y relationship (in light of the scenarios and measurement issues set forth in Chapter 2); (3) visualize variation in the

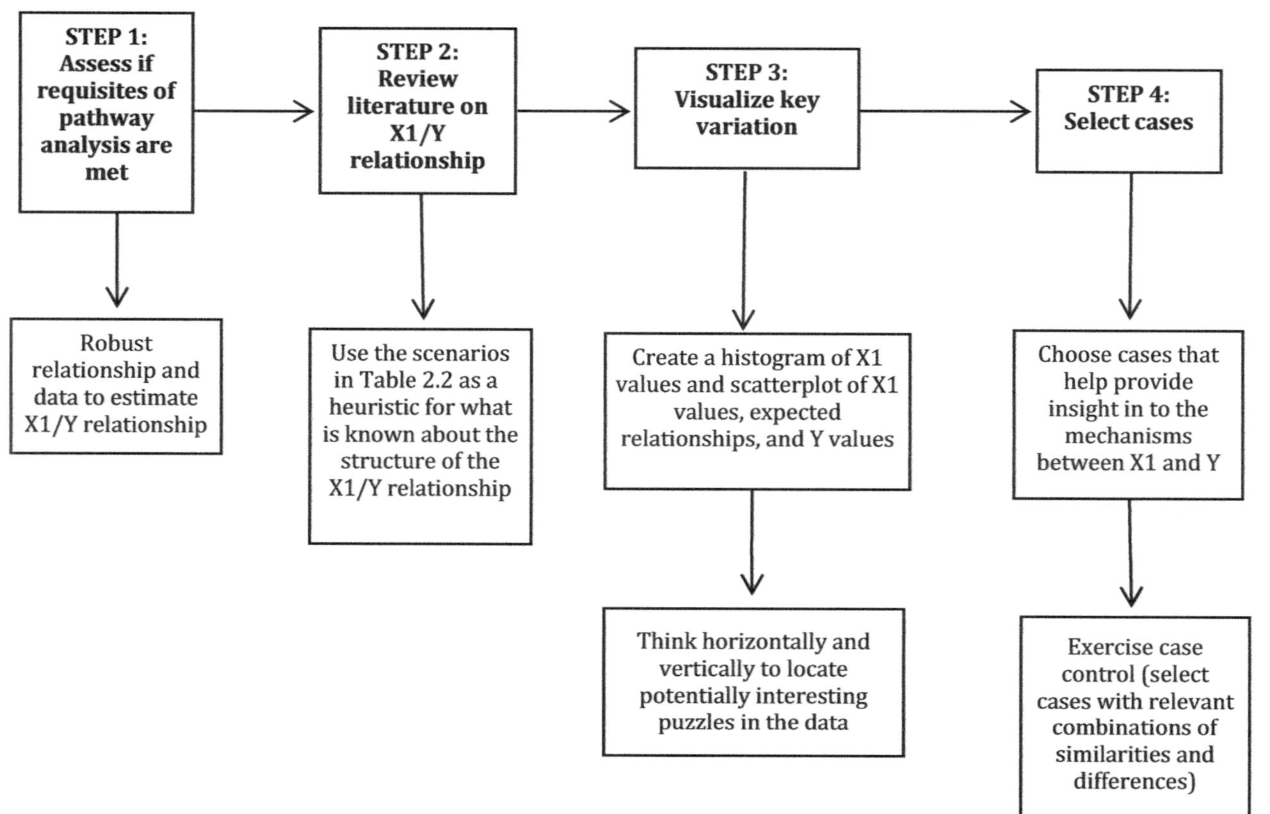

Figure 3.3   Schematic overview of method

data, such as by plotting the X1 values, creating a scatterplot using measures of the expected X1/Y relationship and X1 and Y values and thinking vertically and horizontally to locate interesting variation in the scatterplot; and (4) select cases using case control strategies, such as looking for within-case comparisons.

Chapters 2 and 3 have been abstract on purpose to help focus on the general steps in preparing for pathway analysis and selecting cases without getting mired in the details of specific applications. Our approach will become more meaningful when applied to concrete examples. The following chapters take on that task, with particular emphasis on case selection. In the next chapter we begin by comparing our approach to its main alternatives using several simple, textbook hypotheticals, and then turn to more complex examples drawn from the literatures on policy diffusion and the "curse" of natural resources.

4 Comparison of case selection approaches

4.1 Introduction

The approach we present in this book is not the only way to select
cases for pathway analysis. The literature suggests two alternatives: the
variable-based approach and the residual-based approach. This chapter
reviews these methods, critiques them, and compares their application to our method using several textbook examples drawn from John
Gerring's *Case Study Research: Principles and Practices* (2007). We use
examples from Gerring for several reasons. They are simple and heuristi-
cally useful. These examples have been used to demonstrate the utility of
the prior case selection approaches, and therefore they provide a bench-
mark against which to demonstrate the advantages of our approach. In
subsequent chapters, we apply our approach to more complex examples,
but many of the basic points – such as the need to select comparative
cases, the usefulness of considering both the expected X1/Y relationship
and variation in case characteristics, the utility of visualizing patterns
within the data, and using case control strategies – can be seen even in
this chapter's simple examples.

4.2 Overview of the variable-based approach

The variable-based approach has the advantage of simplicity; it urges
researchers to seek cases with extreme values of X1 and Y (see Seawright
and Gerring 2008). The assumption of this approach is that cases with
large X1 and Y values are most likely to feature the X1/Y relationship

and thus provide a promising case for exploring causal pathways.[1] The values of X1 and Y are potentially useful pieces of information for those interested in pathway analysis, but focusing on the X1 and Y values *alone* is problematic for a number of reasons. First, the variable-based approach does not deal with the problem of potential confounds; it simply assumes a straightforward X1/Y relationship. Second, if we select cases with extreme values of X1 and Y, it is difficult to assess whether these cases are outliers in the absence of a strong theory about the nature of the relationship. Third, the variable-based approach does not account for the underlying functional form of the X1/Y relationship. For example, if the underlying functional form of the X1/Y relationship is an S-shaped curve in which the expected relationship between X1 and Y changes as the values of X1 change, then selecting cases with high X1 values may be counter-productive in terms of our ability to observe mechanisms of interest. The point is not to ignore the values of X1 and Y when selecting cases – this is useful information. A researcher needs to use this information cautiously and in conjunction with other information gleaned from the existing data and studies.

4.2.1 The variable-based approach applied and compared

The central difference between our pathway analysis approach and the variable-based "extreme case" approach can be illustrated by comparing how each is applied to the type of example that seems most suited to the variable-based approach: cases where all variables are coded dichotomously; all independent variables (including X1) and all controls (X2) are positively correlated with Y; and X1 is sufficient by itself to cause Y at least in some instances (Gerring 2007). This type of relationship effectively eliminates the problem of confounds because, given the dichotomous nature of the variables and the fact that

---

[1] This example assumes increases in X1 are associated with increases in Y.

Table 4.1 Case selection with dichotomous
causal variables

Case types	X1	X2	Y
A	1	1	1
B	0	0	0
C	0	1	1
D	0	0	1
E	1	0	0
F	1	1	0
G	0	1	0
H	1	0	1

Source: Gerring (2007).

X1 is sometimes sufficient to cause Y, a researcher can choose cases to eliminate confounds. This type of relationship and measures are promising for the variable-based approach.

Under these circumstances, it is easy to represent the eight possible types of cases in a table, and to label them A through H (see Table 4.1). The variable-based approach points to cases where X1 has a clear relationship with Y. Specifically, researchers would select type H cases, where the relationship of interest occurs and there are no confounders (i.e., X1 and Y = 1 and X2 = 0). In the other seven cases, the X1/Y relationship cannot be easily observed. Either the key variable of interest does not occur (X1 = 0; types B, C, D, and G); the outcome does not occur (Y = 0; types B, E, F, and G); and/or there are possible confounders (X2 = 1; types A, C, F, and G).[2] Following the logic of the variable-based

---

[2] The same general logic would apply if the causes were conjunctural, so that some combination of factors is sufficient, but not necessary, to cause an outcome, as in most Quantitative Comparative Analysis (QCA) models (Ragin 2000). Here, instead of having X1 represent a single variable, it would represent a distinct configuration of variables, and a researcher would want to identify cases where this configuration of variables and the outcome is present but other confounding factors are not (whether single factors or clusters).

Table 4.2 Case selection with dichotomous causal variables where causal mechanism knowledge is limited or uncertain

Does the case feature the key explanatory variable, X1?	Does the case feature the outcome Y (controlling for possible confounds, X2)?	
	Yes	No
Yes	Effect case $(X1 = 1; Y = 1)$	Non-outcome case $(X1 = 1; Y = 0)$
No	Non-effect case $(X1 = 0; Y = 1)$	Control case $(X1 = 0; Y = 0)$

approach, Gerring argues that "an in-depth examination of cases A–G is not likely to be very revealing" (2007: 125).

Our approach requires researchers to select multiple cases that collectively address both the expected relationship and variation in case characteristics. From the perspective of the expected X1/Y relationship, Gerring is clearly right that type H cases are the most interesting and that any case selection should include at least one of this type of case. From the perspective of variation of case characteristics, however, focusing only on type H cases is likely to be a mistake. Unless it is known that there is a single mechanism connecting X1 and Y that acts consistently (see scenario 1, the Single Pathway Scenario, in Chapter 2), then variation in the relationship should be considered and a researcher should select cases that involve different relationships between X1 and Y, controlling for X2. (Of course, if it is already known that only one mechanism exists and that it operates the same regardless of X1 values, then comparative pathway analysis would not seem particularly valuable.) In thinking about choosing cases with interesting variation, there are four types of cases that are of potential interest ($X2 = 0$ in all of these cases) (see Table 4.2):

- effect cases, where $X1 = 1$ and $Y = 1$;
- control cases, where $X1 = 0$ and $Y = 0$;

- non-outcome cases, where X1 = 1 and Y = 0; and
- non-treatment cases where X1 = 0 and Y = 1.

Choosing multiple cases for a comparison can provide better ability to generate hypotheses about causal pathways compared to a narrow focus on effect cases, because it allows a researcher to consider how changes from X1 = 0 to X1 = 1 correspond (or not) to changes in outcomes from Y = 0 to Y = 1.

When knowledge about the X1/Y relationship is uncertain, the primary goal of pathway analysis is to probe the underlying structure of the relationship in light of the scenarios in Chapter 2. To do so, a researcher would want to identify several general avenues of inquiry for case studies, such as the number of likely mechanisms; the relationship among different mechanisms; and the extent to which mechanisms are related to other explanatory variables. For instance, to investigate the existence of multiple mechanisms requires studying multiple cases (especially from the effect and non-outcome categories) to determine if the same combination of mechanisms appears across cases. To understand the relationship between the explanatory variable and mechanism, it would be useful to study effect and non-effect cases to generate hypotheses about whether mechanisms appear even in the absence of the key explanatory variable. If the goal is to focus on the sufficiency of one or more mechanisms, then a researcher would do well to study effect cases, non-outcome cases, and non-effect cases. Comparisons across these three types of cases can help to develop hypotheses about which mechanisms are sufficient for the outcome to occur.

It is worth noting that extending the case selection does not need to involve selecting an entirely new set of cases for cross-case analysis. Instead, researchers can look for within-case comparisons by examining differences within a given unit; for example, in studying war, there may be periods in a country's history that resemble control cases and others that resemble effect cases. This would allow us to observe changes in X1 and to understand the causal mechanisms that X1 manifests (and, along the way, gain some insight into the degree that X1 and related mechanisms co-vary). Alternatively, we might be able to make comparisons across both regions and time within a country such that some regions would resemble control cases and others would resemble effect cases.

The broader point is that case selection should consider both the expected relationship and variation in case characteristics, unless the level of knowledge about mechanisms is already very well developed (which, of course, makes pathway analysis less appropriate in the first place). However, where knowledge of mechanisms is partial or uncertain, it is necessary to adopt a comparative strategy, not an extreme value case strategy. By studying different types of cases, a researcher will be in a better position to hypothesize about the structure of the X1/Y relationship.

There are formal models that generate expectations that roughly fall into this pattern. Consider Jim Fearon's (1995) study about the causes of war. In Fearon's model, the inability of a state to credibly commit to a particular course of action or information asymmetries between two actors could be sufficient causes of war. According to the theory, if neither problem exists, that is, when X1 = 0 and X2 = 0, then the two actors will negotiate a division of any contested, limited resource rather than fight over it, which would reduce its value to both parties. In the presence of commitment problems, however, war can occur. This model provides some insight into the mechanism(s) that might link commitment problems to conflict, but it does not address how one or more mechanisms actually occur and what conditions make such occurrence more or less likely. It is possible that commitment problems can reflect attributes of the state or bottom-up dynamics, as key constituents threaten leadership when they cannot reliably supply critical resources. In the context of this model, there is much to be learned about the precise mechanisms that link a state's credible commitment problems to conflict.

Table 4.3 Case selection for pathway analysis between commitment problems and war over limited resources (when asymmetric information does not exist)

Is there a commitment problem?	Does a country decide to go to war?	
	Yes	No
Yes	Commitment problem and war (effect cases)	Commitment problem but no war (non-outcome cases)
No	No commitment problem and war (non-treatment cases)	No commitment problem and no war (control cases)

Note: Asymmetric information does not exist in any case.

Following the logic of our approach, researchers who want to explore causal pathways between a state's commitment problems and the decision to go to war should adopt a comparative case design. Table 4.3 presents the four types of cases that can be selected based on the presence/absence of commitment problems and whether war occurs or not. Using the nomenclature of this chapter, X1 represents the presence of commitment problems; X2 the presence (or absence) of asymmetric information; and Y whether a war occurs. We suggest selecting cases for pathway analysis aimed at generating hypotheses about how commitment problems are related to the decision to go to war, including hypotheses about the number of mechanisms, co-variation among mechanisms, and if there are mechanisms sufficient to make a commitment problem lead to war. Studying a single type of case would not allow you to address these questions, which is why a comparative approach is essential.

4.3 Overview of the residual-based approach

The residual-based approach is an attempt to address some of the limitations of the variable-based approach, as it focuses on the relationship between X1 and Y, not their values (Gerring 2007). In this approach, the criteria for selecting cases are: (1) the case is not an outlier (or at least an extreme outlier) in the full regression model, and (2) the X1 variable is related to the outcome Y. To assess these criteria, a researcher must analyze the residuals of individual cases in the model after estimating a regression.[3] To test if a case is an outlier, Gerring advises checking if the size of the standardized residual in the full model is very high (greater than |2|).[4] If so, it should be excluded, because it is an outlier and not typical of the estimated relationship (Seawright and Gerring 2008). The residual-based approach focuses on whether the *relationship* between X1 and Y is typical, which differs from whether the selected case's causal mechanisms are typical or generalizable. In the absence of a well-developed theory establishing that a single mechanism acts homogeneously across different levels of effects on the outcome, it is unknown whether a case featuring a "typical" relationship will also feature a "typical" mechanism.

To estimate the relationship between X1 and the outcome using the residual-based method, researchers need to compare the size of the residual in the full model, which includes X1, to the size of the residual in a reduced model, which excludes X1. Using these nested models, the residual-based approach defines an appropriate case as a non-outlier that shows the greatest reduction between the size of residual in the full model and reduced model. The reasoning is straightforward. If the size of the residual in the reduced model is larger than the residual in the full model, the inclusion of X1 leads to a more accurate prediction of the outcome, suggesting that the case features the X1/Y relationship. If the size of the residual in the reduced model is smaller than the full model, then the inclusion of X1 leads to a less accurate prediction of the outcome. Based on this reasoning, Gerring (2007) proposes a formula

---

[3] The residual is the difference between the actual, observed value of the dependent variable and the predicted value of the dependent variable from the regression.

[4] There are other ways to identify whether a case is anomalous using Cook's distance, leverage plots, etc. As always, researchers should conduct appropriate regression diagnostics to ensure that they appropriately understand the X1/Y relationship.

for calculating what he calls the "Pathway Value," which is Pathway Value $= |\mathrm{Res}_{\mathrm{reduce}} - \mathrm{Res}_{\mathrm{full}}|$ if $|\mathrm{Res}_{\mathrm{reduce}}| > |\mathrm{Res}_{\mathrm{full}}|$ (127).

4.3.1   The residual-based approach applied

In his book, Gerring uses a hypothetical based on the "oil curse" literature to illustrate the residual-based approach. This literature identifies a negative relationship between a country's oil wealth (X1) and the level of democracy (Y). The hypothetical posits that there are three potential mechanisms connecting oil wealth and levels of democracy: (1) a rentier effect in which a government uses its mineral wealth to support low taxes and patronage to blunt accountability; (2) a repression effect in which a government uses its mineral wealth to bolster its internal security apparatus; and (3) a modernization effect in which growth based on oil exports fails to engender the social and cultural changes needed to promote democracy. In his discussion, Gerring stresses that these are all speculative claims. It is not known, among other things, whether these mechanisms are exhaustive or exclusive; whether they interact; or whether they function similarly as the amount of oil wealth and its relationship with levels of democracy changes.

Gerring makes matters more concrete by operationalizing oil wealth (X1) as barrels of oil per capita and levels of democracy (Y) using the Polity 2 scale, which ranges from -10 (most authoritarian) to +10 (most democratic). Controls (X2) are added for GDP per capita (logged); Muslims as a percent of the population; European languages spoken; and ethnic fractionalization (the likelihood of two randomly chosen individuals belonging to the same ethnic group). Gerring focuses on nineteen countries across Africa, Asia, Europe, the Middle East, and South America, although there are more countries in the underlying dataset. (For the sake of comparison, we focus on the same subset of cases.) Table 4.4 replicates Gerring's results (2007), which shows the residual for each case from the full and reduced regression models and the difference between the two residuals.

Table 4.4 Pathway Values for oil curse hypothetical

Country	Size of residual in reduced model (without oil wealth)	Size of residual in full model (with oil wealth)	Pathway value (change in residual)
Iran	−0.282	−0.456	0.175
Turkmenistan	−1.220	−1.398	0.178
Mauritania	−0.076	−0.255	0.179
Turkey	2.261	2.069	0.192
Switzerland	0.177	−0.028	0.205
Venezuela	0.148	0.355	−0.207
Belgium	0.518	0.310	0.208
Morocco	−0.540	−0.776	0.236
Jordan	0.384	0.142	0.240
Djibouti	−0.451	−0.696	0.245
Bahrain	−1.411	−1.673	0.262
Luxembourg	0.559	0.291	0.269
Singapore	−1.593	−1.864	0.271
Oman	−1.270	−0.981	−0.289
Gabon	−1.743	−1.418	−0.325
Saudi Arabia	−1.681	−1.253	−0.428
Norway	0.315	1.285	−0.971
United Arab Emirates	−1.256	−0.081	−1.175
Kuwait	−1.007	0.925	−1.932

Note: Replicated from Gerring (2007: 129).

In Gerring's example, some cases are immediately disqualified. Turkey, for example, is an extreme outlier, as its standardized residual in the full model is greater than 2. Others can be removed from consideration because the size of the residual – its absolute value – for the reduced model is less than that of the full model, so that its Pathway Value is negative (e.g., Norway). For these countries, the residual from the regression model is smaller when oil wealth is *excluded* from the model. Among the cases where the Pathway Value is positive, the United Arab Emirates and Kuwait look to be particularly good cases, as they feature large Pathway Values and the residual in the full model is close to 0, so that these cases are well predicted by the statistical model.

4.4 Selecting cases using the pathway analysis approach

There are several limitations to the residual-based approach. For starters, it only directly applies in cases where the residual is a useful concept (i.e., OLS regression). In addition, even if residuals are a useful concept, the formula for Pathway Value needs to be modified. Specifically, assuming the residual is a useful concept, we define the expected relationship in this context as $|\text{Res}_{\text{reduce}}| - |\text{Res}_{\text{full}}|$. The modification of taking the absolute value of the residuals *before* subtracting them reflects the need to account for cases where the size of the residuals are similar but of different signs; for example, if a case has a $\text{Res}_{\text{reduce}}$ of 1.0 and a Res_{full} of -0.9. (i.e., the residuals are of similar sizes but different signs). Under the original formula, its Pathway Value is 1.9. In our modified formula, the expected relationship would be 0.1, which suggests that this case is not particularly strong on this criterion. We also discard the condition that $|\text{Res}_{\text{reduce}}| > |\text{Res}_{\text{full}}|$, because doing so allows us to consider more types of variation in expected relationships when selecting cases. From our perspective, if a particular case has a smaller residual when X1 is excluded then it is interesting to compare that to a case(s) where the residual is larger when X1 is excluded. To see the similarities and differences between our approach and the residual-based approach, it is useful to work through the logic of our approach from beginning to end.

4.4.1 Step 1: Assessing the requisites for pathway analysis

The first step in our approach is to determine whether pathway analysis is appropriate. In the oil wealth example, the hypothetical assumes a robust, negative, and linear relationship between oil wealth and levels of democratization. In addition, relevant data are available for large-N analysis. This meets the basic requisites for pathway analysis.

4.4.2   Step 2: Reviewing the literature on the X1/Y relationship

The next step is to review the literature on the X1/Y relationship in light of the scenarios in Chapter 2 (see Table 2.2). In this hypothetical, knowledge about causal mechanisms is speculative and incomplete. The hypothetical posits multiple mechanisms (equifinality), but it is not clear whether these proposed mechanisms are exhaustive, act discretely or conjointly, interact, or work similarly across different levels of oil wealth, effect sizes, and so on. To use the nomenclature from Chapter 2, a researcher knows that neither the Single Pathway nor the Direct and Indirect Pathway Scenarios apply because there are multiple mechanisms, but does not know whether the pathways are mutually exclusive. As such, there is significant opportunity to use pathway analysis to generate hypotheses about the basic structure of the X1/Y relationship.

4.4.3   Step 3: Visualize key variation

After reviewing the literature, it is time to turn to the data and begin to visualize variation that suggests interesting puzzles to explore. To start, a distributional plot of oil wealth (X1) should be created.

Figure 4.1 is a histogram that presents the distribution of the per capita oil wealth among all of the cases in Gerring's dataset. It is immediately obvious that many countries have no significant oil wealth. The two cases that the variable-based and residual-based approaches identify (Kuwait and United Arab Emirates) are far out on the right-hand side of the distribution of oil wealth, and thus they differ significantly from most of the other cases on this variable. Given the general lack of knowledge about the underlying mechanisms – when they occur, how they function, whether they interact – it is unknown if *any* case will

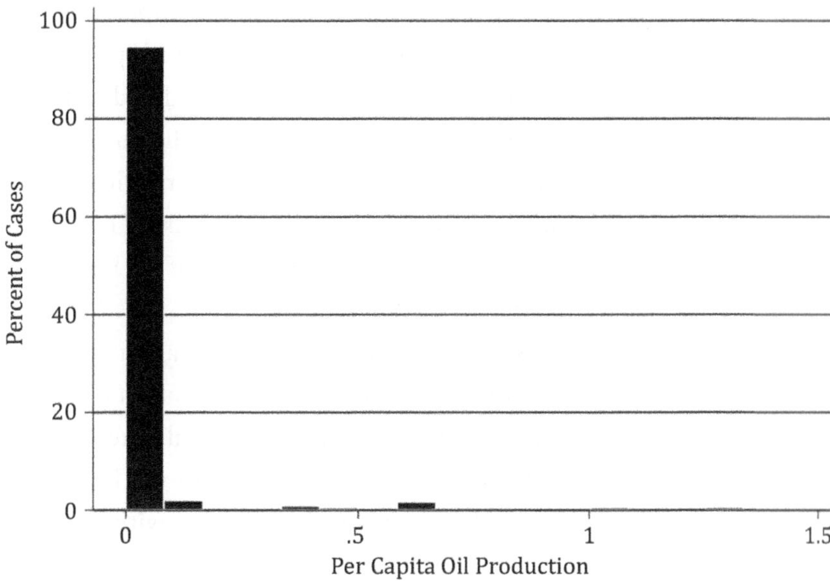

Figure 4.1   Distribution of per capita oil production

feature mechanisms that are representative of the unobserved set of cases. However, given the differences in the levels of oil wealth, researchers should be particularly wary about applying knowledge from cases of high oil wealth to other cases. At the very least, the researcher needs to consider if the mechanisms observed in these cases are likely to apply in other settings with less oil wealth – something that the other approaches, which focus on finding individual cases with extreme values of the key variables or Pathway Value, tend to miss.

Once there is a sense of the distribution of X1 values in the sample, the work can turn to assessing the expected relationship and how the estimated case-level relationship between oil wealth (X1) and levels of democracy (Y) varies, controlling for other factors.[5] Given the

---

[5] The expected relationship estimated via comparing residuals is not equivalent to an individual-level causal effect. Rather, the expected relationship is a way to identify the cases for which knowledge of the key explanatory variable improves our ability to predict the outcome. Further, using the residuals approach assumes that if

functional form of the relationship, a comparison of residuals is a reasonable way to assess the expected relationships in different cases (alternatives to comparing residuals are considered in later chapters). However, the modified formula must be applied to determine the expected relationship. The scores for the expected relationship are represented in Table 4.5. Note that the expected relationship for Kuwait sharply differs from its Pathway Value because the size of the residual with and without oil is similar but has different signs.

With this information, a researcher can visualize key aspects of the data by creating a scatterplot of the variation in the expected relationship, the level of oil wealth, and the actual outcome. Figure 4.2 plots the expected relationship on the y-axis and the level of oil wealth on the x-axis. Selected observations are labeled with the country's name and Polity 2 score (i.e., the outcome).

Using Figure 4.2, patterns emerge by thinking horizontally and vertically, as discussed in Chapter 3. Thinking horizontally means looking for interesting patterns of cases based on the X1 values, and we see there are cases with high levels of oil wealth (greater than 1), medium levels of oil wealth (between 0.3 and 0.7), and low levels (less than 0.2). Thinking vertically, among the cases with high, medium, and low amounts of oil wealth, there is variation with respect to both the expected relationship and observed values of Y. Combining cases drawn from different regions in the data provides an opportunity to explore a variety of questions related to the structure of the X1/Y relationship.

One avenue of inquiry is to compare the United Arab Emirates to Kuwait, because both cases have similarly high levels of oil wealth and low democracy scores, yet the expected relationship sharply differs.

knowledge of that variable improves our predictions in a case then such a case will be more likely to feature the causal mechanism than in cases where knowledge of the key explanatory variable does not improve our predictions. In the absence of knowledge about how the observable large-N data relate to the unobserved causal mechanisms, even a valid measure of individual level causal effects may not tell us which cases actually feature the mechanisms.

Table 4.5 Expected relationships for oil curse

Country	Absolute value of residual in reduced model (without oil wealth)	Absolute value of residual in full model (with oil wealth)	Expected relationship (change in size of residual)
United Arab Emirates	1.256	0.081	1.175
Saudi Arabia	1.681	1.253	0.428
Gabon	1.743	1.418	0.325
Oman	1.27	0.981	0.289
Luxembourg	0.559	0.291	0.268
Jordan	0.382	0.142	0.24
Belgium	0.518	0.31	0.208
Turkey	2.261	2.069	0.192
Switzerland	0.177	0.028	0.149
Kuwait	1.007	0.925	0.082
Iran	0.282	0.456	−0.174
Turkmenistan	1.22	1.398	−0.178
Mauritania	0.076	0.255	−0.179
Venezuela	0.148	0.355	−0.207
Morocco	0.54	0.776	−0.236
Djibouti	0.451	0.696	−0.245
Bahrain	1.411	1.673	−0.262
Singapore	1.593	1.864	−0.271
Norway	0.315	1.285	−0.97

Note: Based on Gerring (2007). A positive expected relationship means that the regression that includes oil wealth, the key explanatory variable, has a smaller residual than the regression without it.

Why is it that both cases have considerable oil wealth but only one, the United Arab Emirates, features the expected relationship? Is some mechanism present in the United Arab Emirates but not in Kuwait? Are there other mechanisms in Kuwait that lead to low levels of democracy regardless of oil wealth? Exploring these types of questions using in-depth case analysis would allow a researcher to explore a number of critical issues related to the structure of the X1/Y relationship, including:

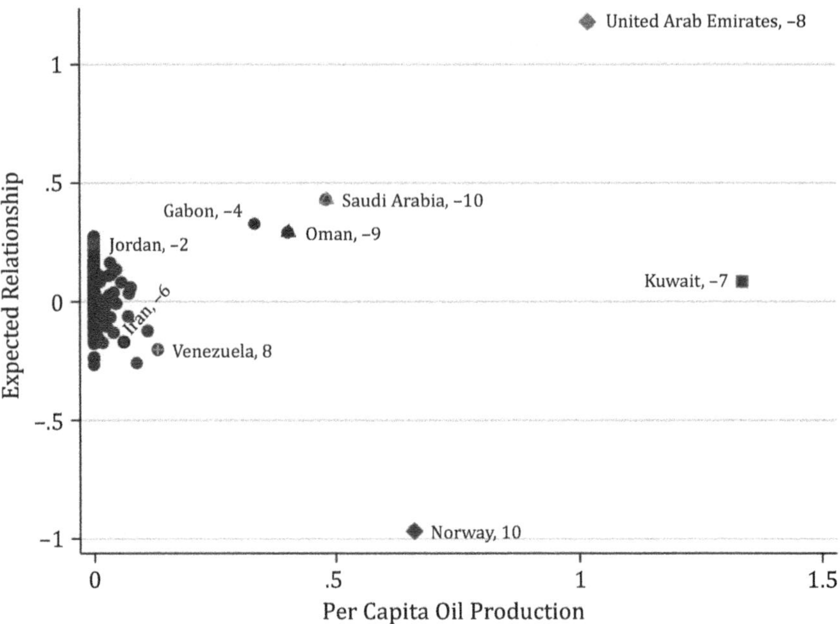

Figure 4.2   Visualizing key variation: expected relationship, oil production, and name of country with Polity score

- whether there are multiple mechanisms;
- whether certain mechanisms appear in some cases but not others;
- whether some mechanisms appear in the absence of the treatment or cancel each other out;
- whether certain mechanisms (or combinations of them) are sufficient to achieve the outcome; and
- whether there are other factors associated with key mechanisms.

Note that the residual-based approach might also lead a researcher to choose Kuwait and the United Arab Emirates. However, a researcher using that approach would expect these countries to be "likely" cases for observing the X1/Y relationship and might be tempted to draw an incorrect inference from the lack of relationship in the Kuwait case. Our approach avoids that pitfall.

Visualizing the data in this way also helps underscore a downside of comparing only Kuwait and the United Arab Emirates as suggested by the residual-based approach; namely, their levels of oil wealth are anomalous, which raises questions about their generalizability to other cases in the sample given the limited amount of knowledge about mechanisms in the hypothetical. As a result, in addition to comparing these cases, it would be prudent to look at cases with lower (and thus more typical) levels of oil wealth. Here too the data suggest a number of interesting puzzles, as cases with medium levels of oil wealth also feature a significant range of expected relationships. Saudi Arabia, Oman, and Gabon all have similar levels of oil wealth, positive expected relationships, and negative Polity 2 scores, while Norway has more oil but the expected relationship is negative. Why does Norway buck the trend? Is there a mechanism that blocks the "oil curse"? Is the oil curse inapplicable to Norway? If so, what does this suggest about the analytic boundaries of the oil curse? Again, comparing cases that have similar oil wealth but differ in their expected relationships and outcomes may give some purchase on generating hypotheses related to the underlying structure of the X1/Y relationship. Because the expected relationship is lower in cases like Saudi Arabia, Oman, and Gabon than the United Arab Emirates, however, we may be concerned that the mechanisms underlying the X1/Y relationship will be harder to observe. As such, we suggest that these comparisons should be combined with an analysis of the United Arab Emirates and Kuwait cases, adding the additional leverage stemming from variation in levels of oil wealth.

Extending this logic, it would be interesting to add cases with low (or no) levels of oil wealth and varying levels of democracy, such as Jordan, Iran, or Venezuela. Obviously, these cases standing alone cannot be used to probe the relationship between oil wealth and democratization, because they have little oil wealth. However, adding these countries allows comparison of cases with varying levels of X1, Y values, and expected relationships. This provides an opportunity to study what happens as cases transition across these dimensions, from cases without oil wealth to oil wealth, and seeing how this relates to shifts in levels of democracy and the effects of oil wealth. This would allow a researcher to consider, among other things, whether some mechanisms appear in the absence of oil wealth, or some mechanisms are more likely to appear at different levels of X1 or relationships with Y, or some mechanisms are associated with other explanatory variables.

4.4.4   Step 4: Selecting cases

Researchers typically can only study a limited number of cases given the demanding nature of thorough qualitative work. In making any final decisions about which cases to examine, researchers should look for opportunities to exercise case control. Depending on the research question, it may be useful to capitalize on the fact that many of the oil wealth cases are in the Middle East. Such geographic proximity might facilitate comparisons, thereby allowing researchers to contrast cases that share values of key variables and examine why similar cases seem to engender different effects. Conversely, researchers might want to take advantage of the geographic diversity in the cases and select countries from different regions that exhibit similar effects. While adopting case control strategies will not ensure that any of these cases represent "typical" mechanisms, they do allow for exploration of the functioning of mechanisms among cases where the level of oil wealth and the expected relationship varies, which seems a better basis for generating hypotheses than examining critical cases with extreme values using the variable- or residual-based approaches. Of course, we recognize that researchers may not be able to include all of these cases for practical reasons, or they may plan to study some countries for practical or theoretical reasons and need to place these cases into context. Applying our approach allows for a better understanding of the trade-offs inherent in whatever choices are made; this is something that an extreme case approach (whether based on the values of the key measures or an analysis of residuals) is unlikely to do.

The bottom line is that considering expected relationships and variations in case characteristics – in combination with any relevant preexisting theoretical or substantive knowledge about the cases and promising case control strategies – reveals opportunities for comparisons that might be overlooked from the perspective of other approaches. These comparisons, in turn, provide a better foundation than cases with extreme values for building plausible hypotheses about the structure of the X1/Y relationship. Researchers might focus on exploring the number of mechanisms, how they interact with each other and the treatment, their possible sufficiency and observational equivalence, and whether they function similarly across variation in cases.

4.5   Summary

This chapter compared our method to others, and demonstrated how our approach suggests the selection of different cases when applied to the same examples using the same data. The most important difference is our emphasis on *comparison*. Specifically, to understand causal mechanisms requires selecting cases based on both the expected relationships and variations in case characteristics using information about the values of key variables *and* the relationship in individual cases.

A critical point is that applying these principles depends on knowledge of the expected relationship between X1 and Y; the nature of the outcome; and the state of knowledge about causal pathways, which is often limited and uncertain. This means that researchers cannot take a mechanical approach to selecting cases. Instead, they must build a flexible tool kit for assessing the expected X1/Y relationship and case variation and be aware of the limits of using different tools when interpreting the results of their case studies.

Finally, selecting cases based on the expected X1/Y relationship and variation in case characteristics does not guarantee that a researcher will observe "typical" mechanisms, or even any mechanisms at all, though the quantitative data can provide useful information about the distribution of the X1 variable and the expected X1/Y relationship. These bits of information can reveal interesting puzzles – such as why some cases have similar X1 values and expected relationships but different outcomes – that will lead to probing of the X1/Y relationship across settings. Ultimately, it is the work of case studies to fill in the unobserved links between the variables; effective case selection can only point to promising puzzles to study. Exploring these puzzles will provide a reasonable basis for generating hypotheses about the basic structure of the X1/Y relationship, such as the number of mechanisms, whether mechanisms interact and co-vary with variables and outcomes, and whether mechanisms function similarly across different levels of effect. All of these types of insights can significantly contribute to a researcher's understanding of the X1/Y relationship, which is the primary goal of pathway analysis.

5 Regression-based case selection for pathway analysis of non-linear relationships

5.1 Introduction

In the last chapter, we applied our method to several simple textbook examples, including a hypothetical that posited a linear X1/Y relationship with equifinality (that is, multiple pathways between X1 and Y). In this chapter, we turn to a discussion of case selection in a more complex empirical setting: one that features a non-linear relationship between X1 and Y and the relationship is embedded in a longer causal chain that involves dynamic processes.[1] Under these conditions, researchers must decide where in the causal process to investigate and how to deal with temporal dynamics in their large- and small-N studies. This chapter grapples with these issues by using an example drawn from the policy diffusion literature. As we make clear, in the context of pathway analysis, conceptualizing what is the key explanatory variable and what is the mechanism is not determined by the labels used in prior research or deep

---

[1] Establishing the functional form of the relationship between X1 and Y is a necessary component of a large-N pathway analysis, because it is only with a significant number of observations that the form of the X1/Y relationship can be accurately identified. With a small number of data points, many possible functional forms might fit the data. However, with additional observations in a large sample of data, the increased number of data points constrains the possible functional form, so a researcher may be relatively confident in determining the actual functional form. Once the existence of a robust correlation between X1 and Y and the functional form of the relationship has been established, then a researcher can begin to carefully select the case(s) for pathway analysis.

philosophical concerns, but rather by practical concerns regarding the relevant research question, how variables are used within the existing empirical research, and data availability. Once the relevant literature is properly understood, our method can be applied in a relatively straight-forward manner.

5.2   International policy diffusion

The literature on international policy diffusion is both immense and contested. For purposes of this chapter, therefore, we distinguish between two very different types of studies. One type focuses on the threshold question of whether policy choices spread across political boundaries; that is, whether policy adoption is purely a function of domestic pressures (Berry and Berry 1990; Gray 1973, 1994; Simmons et al. 2008; cf. Volden et al. 2008). The second type of study essentially assumes that policies diffuse across borders, so its focus is on how and under what conditions policy decisions of one country spill over into others. In general, the literature that assumes the existence of diffusion and focuses on how policy diffusion works is more interesting for our purposes, as the search for mechanisms lies at its center (Simmons et al. 2008).

To make things more manageable, we focus on Beth A. Simmons and Zachary Elkins' (2004) article, "The Globalization of Liberalization: Policy Diffusion in the International Political Economy," which is a study of international policy diffusion of liberal and restrictive economic policies between 1967 and 1996. A number of features make this article appropriate for our purposes. First, as of the writing of this book, the article has been cited more than 800 times on Google Scholar, so it is clearly influential in the study of cross-national policy diffusion.[2] Second, it has a publicly available dataset that makes it possible for us to

---

[2] Citation count was as of February 5, 2014.

apply our case selection technique. Third, the authors developed large-N empirical measures related to the study of diffusion, which gives us a chance to work through how pathway analysis might be used to probe the validity of large-N measures. Finally, it raises a number of interesting case selection challenges because the empirical relationship described by Simmons and Elkins depends on cross-sectional *and* temporal causal processes that create a complex causal chain. This forces us to wrestle with how to conceptualize variables and mechanisms and how to develop some practical strategies for accounting for both cross-sectional and temporal processes in large- and small-N research methods.

5.2.1   Step 1: Assessing the requisites of pathway analysis

The first step of our approach requires assessing if there is an X1/Y relationship worth exploring and, if so, whether there are data to which we can apply our method. The short answer is that Simmons and Elkins' article meets our threshold criteria; otherwise, why else choose it for analysis? However, the process of reaching this answer is far more complicated than examples in earlier chapters, where the X1/Y relationship was fairly self-explanatory.

To understand this complexity and the lessons to be learned from Simmons and Elkins, we must take a closer look at their argument. In the basic diffusion framework, the key explanatory variable is the policy choices made by other governments; or, as they state, "the decision to liberalize (or restrict) by some governments influences the choices made by others" (Simmons and Elkins 2004: 171–72). They do not directly interrogate this claim, but rather accept that there is a relationship between the behavior of country A and country B, and the substantive question is how this relationship occurs.

In that context, Simmons and Elkins develop theoretical arguments about the ways that policy adoptions might spread between countries. The crux of their contribution to international policy diffusion is to identify the characteristics that make a country either more or less likely

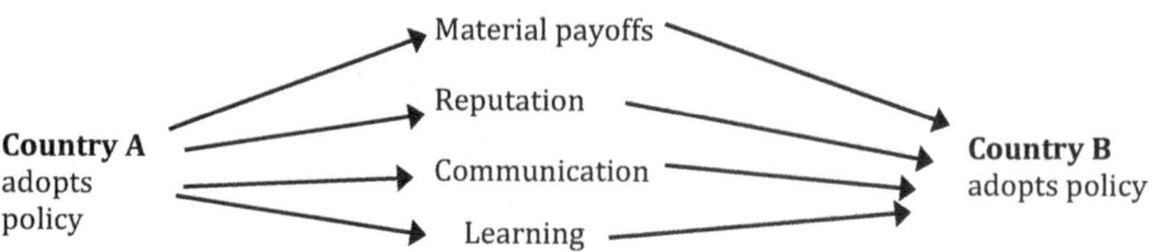

Note: Mechanisms fully mediate relationships between country A and country B.

Figure 5.1   Mechanisms between country A and country B in policy diffusion (according to Simmons and Elkins 2004)

to influence the behavior of another country. The four possible mechanisms of policy diffusion as considered by Simmons and Elkins are outlined in Figure 5.1, and these mechanisms fall into two general categories: altered payoffs or information. Within the category of altered payoffs, the authors' focus is on changes in material (competition for trade and capital) and reputational payoffs; and in the category of information, the authors' focus is on communication between nations and learning from cultural referents. As an example, if countries A and B compete for capital from investors, and country A adopts a liberal economic policy, that should increase the probability that country B will also adopt a liberal economic policy. On the other hand, if countries A and B do not compete for capital, then the decision by country A to adopt a liberal economic policy should not affect country B, assuming that other mechanisms are also absent. The empirical results in their article are centered on using large-N regressions to identify if there is a relationship between what they term a mechanism and the adoption of a particular economic policy.

For convenience, we do not focus on all of the different potential mechanisms related to policy adoption, and instead focus on the relationship between the policies of capital competitors[3] and why a country does or does not adopt liberal capital policies. This relationship appears

---

[3] A country's capital competitors are the other countries that compete with it for foreign capital.

to be the most consistent based on Simmons and Elkins' empirical results and, therefore, is most appropriate for our pathway analysis because the X1/Y relationship seems the most reliable.

Our choice to interrogate this particular step in the causal process, however, implies treating the policies of capital competitors as a key explanatory variable, not as a "mechanism," as Simmons and Elkins do. Therefore we use their data only to guide our selection of cases for pathway analysis, where X1 is the adoption of liberal policies among capital competitors and the Y is the probability of adopting a liberal policy. Based on their article, the mechanisms between these variables are unknown.

Admittedly, this represents a reinterpretation of the *language* of their article, but we believe it does little to change the *substance* of their argument. It is critical to remember, as stated earlier in this book, that there is no single, unified definition of mechanism. In the context of multi-method research, mechanisms are analogous to intervening variables. The question then is not what something is called in a particular study, but rather how it fits within the broader arguments about policy diffusion and how it is treated in analyses. From this perspective, treating Simmons and Elkins' mechanism as a key explanatory variable is reasonable. Despite using the term "mechanism," they neither perform causal mediation analysis nor discuss how someone might disentangle the four purported mechanisms from the general, aggregated effect of policy adoption by other countries. Rather, in their empirical work, they focus on estimating via large-N methods the relationship between the mechanisms they identify and the outcome of interest; that is, whether a country adopts liberal economic policies. Given the data they utilize and their research approach, these mechanisms are better thought of as multiple explanatory variables that affect the behavior of a state, and from which we can develop our strategies for comparative pathway analysis.

The broader lesson is that researchers need to assess carefully an underlying X1/Y relationship. Given the contested nature of the definition of the term mechanism, it is important to drill beneath the surface of the broad literature to see how various factors are used and to identify how an existing large-N analysis lays the foundation for pathway analysis. This is an analytical process, not a mechanical one.

5.2.2   Step 2: Reviewing the literature on the X1/Y relationship

The next step is to assess what is already known about an X1/Y relationship. In this case, if we consider the capital competitors' variable to be the key explanatory variable, then we lack knowledge about the underlying mechanisms that connect a capital competitor's policy to a country's decision to change its own capital policy. Does the decision reflect external factors, such as pressure from international lenders? Internal pressure from constituencies within the country pushing for greater liberalization? Some combination of external and internal factors? In the language of this book's Chapter 2, we do not know which scenario applies to the relationship between capital competitors and liberal policy adoption:

- Scenario 1: Single Pathway;
- Scenario 2: Direct and Indirect Pathways;
- Scenario 3: Multiple Exclusive Pathways; or
- Scenario 4: Multiple Non-Exclusive Pathways.

Under these circumstances, the primary goal of pathway analysis is to generate basic insights into the X1/Y relationship, focusing on the following issues: (1) identifying possible mechanisms that connect capital competitors' policies to a country's change in its policy; (2) investigating whether these mechanisms are independent from each other; and (3) identifying whether the large-N measure of a key explanatory variable is a valid measure of the theoretical construct.

To elaborate briefly, the first and, in this case, most important goal is to build knowledge about the mechanisms that connect capital competitors' policy choices to a country's adoption (or not) of a liberal capital account policy. Because we know little about the mechanisms, an initial purpose of our pathway analysis is to build knowledge about their observable implications. For instance, if a country's policy choice is affected by the policy adoptions of a capital competitor, what might we expect to observe? Would this be revealed by legislative histories? Newspaper accounts? Statements by government officials or business leaders?

A second goal involves building knowledge of what causes the mechanisms, the number of mechanisms, and how (if at all) they interact with one another. Simmons and Elkins provide some insight into the potential interaction between mechanisms when they note that "networks of influence tend to overlap. For example, countries that are geographically clustered are likely to also be important trade partners, competitors, and cultural peers. The correlations across the four diffusion variables range from −0.03 to 0.43" (Simmons and Elkins 2004: 181–82).[4] This is an important piece of information, because if the different explanatory variables from their original study are correlated, then we might observe a mechanism in a given case that is actually caused by one of the other explanatory variables that also occurred in that case. For example, if a country is influenced by the policies of both their capital competitors and trade competitors, then we might ask if there are mechanisms that are unique to each type of competition, or whether the two explanatory variables lead to the same mechanisms. This knowledge is important for understanding the substance of the X1/Y relationship.

Another important avenue of inquiry is whether there are multiple mechanisms associated with the capital competitors' variable, and, if

---

[4] In the context of sequential ignorability, this may suggest the use of sensitivity analysis, but it is unclear what role pathway analysis plays in such a situation. See Chapter 8 for further discussion of this issue.

so, whether different mechanisms can occur at the same time. If the mechanisms are not mutually exclusive (that is, more than one can occur at a time), then we may need to understand whether they have an additive relationship or a more complex relationship in which they interact with each other (and if the interactions happen either all the time or only sometimes). Understanding whether or not the mechanisms interact with one another is an important aspect of identifying which of the scenarios in Table 2.1 (see Chapter 2) best describes this research setting.

A third important topic for pathway analysis is to address the validity of the empirical measures developed by Simmons and Elkins. The large-N results depend on the quality of the underlying empirical measures, and therefore we can be more confident in the results if we can ensure that the measures are reasonable, given the underlying constructs. Of course, conducting a pathway analysis of this type requires us to identify and defend the empirical implications of the relevant variables and mechanism(s) before conducting the analysis. This is a crucial prerequisite for investigations of measurement validity.

Overall, case selection for measurement validity requires that a researcher examine cases in which the underlying construct is expected to be present *and* other cases where it is expected to be absent. Both types of cases are important, because if a quantitative measure suggests the absence of a construct, then the same thing should be found in pathway analysis; and if the quantitative measure suggests the presence of a construct, then a researcher should find case study evidence for it. Unless both types of cases are sampled, a researcher cannot answer whether the quantitative measure accurately identifies both the absence and presence of a construct. This exercise is predicated on the assumption that if research cannot find empirical evidence consistent with large-N measures in a small number of intensively studied cases, then large-N data are likely inaccurate. This seems reasonable because case studies begin with prior knowledge about the likelihood of finding a particular construct, so researchers should find evidence of it if it exists – or fail to find evidence should it not exist. This approach relies upon choosing a set of cases in which the large-N evidence suggests that the construct should be absent in some cases and present in others. In other words, a valid large-N measure should be accurate for cases in which the construct is both present and absent.

If cases are selected to reflect both the expected presence and absence of the construct, this leads to four possible types of observations, as shown in Table 2.3 in Chapter 2. If the cases that are studied fall into the grey-shaded boxes, then it would increase confidence in the large-N measures. However, if pathway analysis fails to confirm the expectations from the large-N data, then it calls the measures into question. However, given that pathway analysis will study only a small number of cases, a researcher cannot determine how pervasive measurement problems may be, but the cases would justify further analysis of the measurement issues.

<table>
<tr><td>5.2.3</td><td>

Step 3: Visualize key variations in data

</td></tr>
</table>

Before demonstrating how to visualize data and select cases in this setting, we need to discuss briefly the large-N analysis conducted by Simmons and Elkins. In their empirical analysis an observation is a country-year, and the dependent variable is whether a country adopted a liberal capital account policy in any year between 1967 and 1996. For the sake of this chapter and our empirical examples, we focus on the relationship between the policies of capital competitors and a country's probability of adopting a liberal capital account policy.[5] To identify which countries competed for capital with each other, Simmons and Elkins group "countries by their yearly Standard and Poor's sovereign

---

[5] Conceptually it is possible to focus on correlations between combinations or configurations of variables and the outcome; however, the additional challenges associated with understanding the interactions between multiple independent variables make both selecting cases and interpreting the findings quite difficult.

bond rating and calculate the mean policy score (for each policy area) for a country's rating category for that year" (Simmons and Elkins 2004: 179). This provides them with a country-by-country measure of the capital account policies of a country's capital competitors. The authors argue that if countries observe that their capital competitors adopt liberal economic policies, then they have an incentive to also adopt liberal policies in the competition for scarce capital. To estimate the relationship between capital competitors' policy choices and a country's own policy choice, the authors use an event history approach, which examines how the different independent variables are correlated with the hazard of an event occurring. This approach is equivalent to grouped binary time-series, cross-sectional data. In our analysis, we took advantage of this equivalence to utilize a logit model with cubic splines to account for temporal issues (Beck et al. 1998). We did this primarily as a matter of convenience, as it makes the approach in this chapter more consistent with the approach we discuss in Chapter 7.

We begin with a basic replication of the results from Simmons and Elkins' article. In Table 5.1 we present both the full (including the capital competitors' variable) and reduced (excluding the capital competitors' variable) empirical models. The full model also demonstrates the positive relationship between the adoption of a liberal capital policy by competitor countries and the probability that an individual country adopts a liberal capital policy. As an aside, we achieved the same statistical significance as Simmons and Elkins, although the coefficient values differ as a result of using the logit model rather than an event history model.

Using the two regressions from Table 5.1, we computed both the predicted probability of adopting a liberal capital policy with the capital competitors' variable (the full model) and the predicted probability of adopting liberal capital policy without the capital competitors' variable (the reduced model). From these two regressions we computed each case's expected relationship between X1 and Y. To do this, for each case we subtracted the predicted probability of the reduced model from the

Table 5.1 Replication of results for diffusion of liberal capital policy

	Full model	Reduced model
Policies of capital competitors	0.83 (0.17)**	–
Policies of trade competitors	0.58 (0.27)*	0.58 (0.25)*
Mean global policy	3.48 (2.23)	3.86 (2.16)
Policies of high growth countries	–0.33 (0.39)	–0.26 (0.38)
Policies of trade partners	0.007 (0.14)	0.003 (0.13)
Policies of BIT partners	–0.30 (0.09)**	–0.34 (0.086)**
Policies of PTA partners	–0.19 (0.18)	–0.25 (0.17)
Policies of religion partners	0.65 (0.26)**	0.58 (0.22)**
Politics of colonial partners	–0.62 (0.59)	–0.68 (0.56)
Policies of language partners	–0.17 (0.12)	–0.14 (0.13)
Current account/GDP (t–2)	0.004 (0.02)	0.007 (0.02)
GDP growth	–0.03 (0.03)	–0.014 (0.038)
GDP per capita	–0.16 (0.05)**	–0.007 (0.04)
World interest rates	0.16 (0.014)	0.10 (0.15)
Currency crisis (t–1)	0.90 (0.49)	0.77 (0.47)
Degree of openness	1.69 (0.51)**	1.47 (0.49)**
Democracy	0.12 (0.08)	0.14 (0.08)
Nationalist executive	N/A[†]	N/A
Central bank independence	0.37 (0.69)	–0.02 (0.57)
Common law legal tradition	–0.77 (0.68)	–0.69 (0.67)
Use of IMF credits	0.29 (0.72)	0.43 (0.78)
Foreign aid (per capita)	–0.02 (0.007)**	–0.012 (0.005)**
Policies of border countries	0.049 (0.58)	0.013(0.065)*
Policies of neighbors	0.33 (0.57)	0.006 (0.55)
Number of observations	2,127	2,127

Note: * = significant at 0.05 level; ** = significant at 0.01 level; [†] Simmons and Elkins included a variable for the presence of a national executive, but values of that variable perfectly predicted the failure to adopt a liberal capital policy in the logit model positive; as a result, this regression has 379 fewer observations than Simmons and Elkins' analysis. Regression includes four cubic splines based on time at risk of failure. Each regression also includes liberalization of current account and exchange rate policies, the other two dependent variables studied by Simmons and Elkins.

predicted probability of the full model; and this difference is our measure of the expected relationship. If the predicted probability is higher in the model that includes the capital competitors' variable, then our measure of expected relationship will be positive; whereas if the predicted probability is higher in the reduced model, then the expected relationship will be negative. Some cases will have a positive expected relationship even though a liberal capital policy was not adopted in that case. This allows us to identify cases in which the estimated relationship differs from the actual outcome (i.e., cases in which the full model predicts a greater probability of the outcome than the reduced model, but the outcome does not occur).

Before we turn to actual case selection, it is necessary to first examine the distribution of the key explanatory variable – in this case, the policies of capital competitors. This preliminary step is important to understand how the key explanatory variable is distributed, which helps us see where most of our data exist and, accordingly, how the selected cases compare to the other cases in our sample on the key explanatory variable. In other words, this preliminary step ensures that we fully understand the large-N data that underpin the selection of our small-N case study. In Figure 5.2, we display a histogram of the capital competitors' variable for each observation in the dataset regardless of whether a country adopted a liberal capital policy in any given year.

A few things jump out about the distribution of the key independent variable:

- The vast bulk of observations have values of policies of capital competitors that fall between 1.6 and 2.2. This implies that in terms of the representativeness of the cases, we would do well to select some cases from this area to help us think through the relevant questions in cases that, based on X1 values, are similar to many other cases.
- There are very few observations with large values for the policies of capital competitors. Therefore, case selection techniques based on

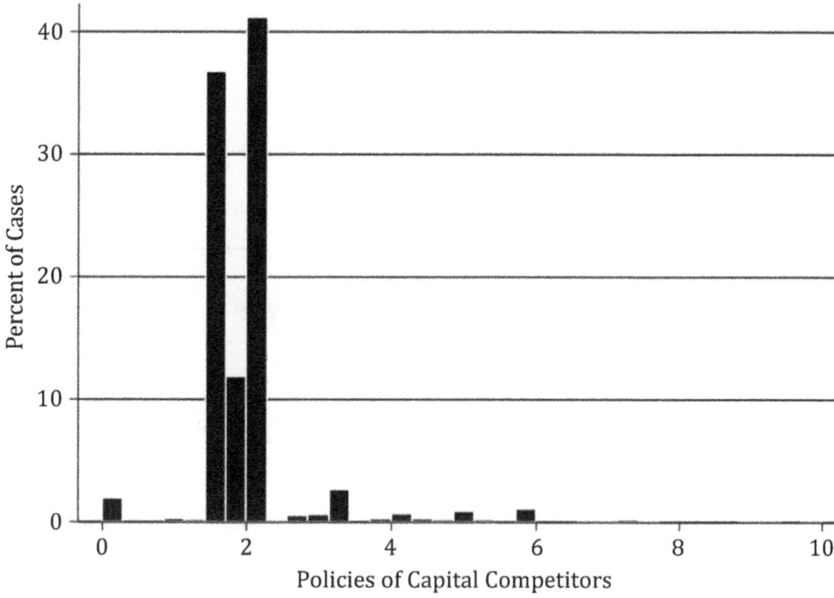

Figure 5.2   Distribution of capital competitors' policy

choosing cases that are extreme on this variable could lead us to pick
cases that are unlike the bulk of the sample of cases.

- The few observations clustered at extreme values of the independent
variable mostly come from the same few countries.

To visualize both the expected relationship and variation in case characteristics across the sample of cases included in the large-N results,
we created Figure 5.3, which on the x-axis plots the value for the key
explanatory variable (policies of capital competitors) and on the y-axis
the difference in the predicted probability of adopting capital liberalization between the full and reduced models (i.e., the expected relationship). The values above 0 on the y-axis indicate that the estimated
probability of policy change is greater in the full model than in the
reduced model (i.e., including the value of the capital competitors' variable is associated with a higher probability of liberal policy adoption).
The observations marked with an "x" represent cases that did adopt

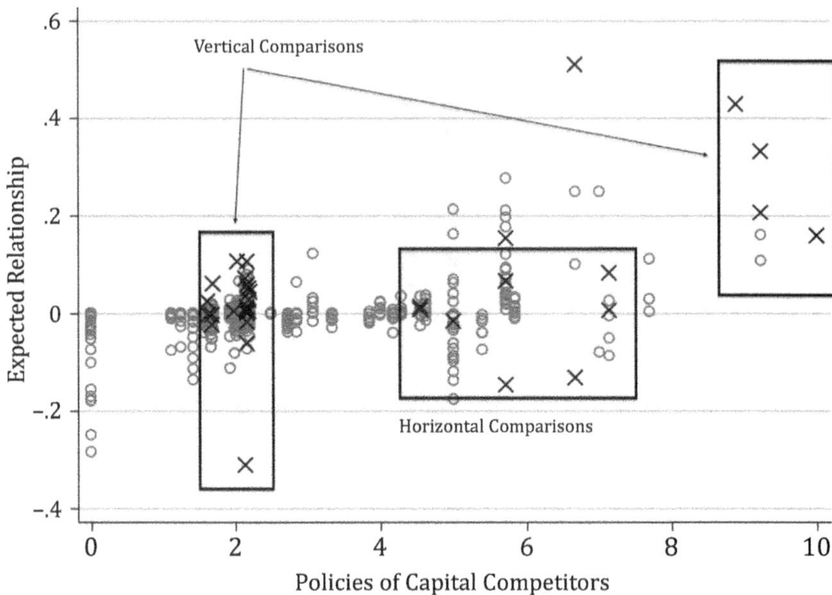

Note: ○ = non-outcome case   × = outcome case

Figure 5.3   Expected relationship and policies of capital competitors

liberal capital policies in a particular year, and the observations marked with dots represent cases that did not adopt liberal capital policies that year. The theoretical maximum for the expected relationship is 1, which implies that a country's probability of adopting liberal capital policies is 0 in the model that excludes the key explanatory variable, and 1 in the model that includes the variable for that mechanism. However, in actuality the maximum score for the expected relationship is ~0.5 (Portugal in 1994). Overall, there are only a few observations in which the value for the estimated relationship is greater than 0.2. This is not a surprise given that in the entire dataset there are 3,280 observations, yet there are only a total of 53 times that countries adopted a liberal capital policy in a given year. Therefore, the baseline adoption rate of capital account liberalization is quite low.

In examining Figure 5.3, a few things emerge from looking for vertical and horizontal comparisons, as recommended earlier in this book. First, we realized that the cases with the highest expected relationship tend to have values of the key independent variable that are far removed from the bulk of the data. This could pose a challenge for us in identifying cases in which we could both observe the mechanism and have confidence that the lessons learned from these cases would apply to others in the dataset. Second, among cases with similar expected relationships, we see both cases that adopt and fail to adopt the outcome. This is important to know because studying cases such as this may shed light on a variety of questions regarding the conditions under which the mechanism is associated with the outcome being studied. Third, there are cases that feature both low values for the expected relationship and small values of the key variable, yet these countries adopted liberal capital policies. Overall, the results displayed in Figure 5.3 suggest that we can identify interesting vertical and horizontal comparisons for our pathway analyses.

5.2.4   Step 4: Selecting the cases

Once we develop a sense of the variation in the X1 variable and the expected relationship, we can then select cases that shed light on substantive research questions. In the context of policy diffusion, we may want to focus on comparisons related to the role that time plays, because it is over time that changes will be seen in the key explanatory variable's value for a given country. In addition, selecting multiple time periods from the same country to study over time may allow us to draw insights from both comparing the case to itself and comparing the case to other cases (either in the same region or the same time period).

The first question that occurs is: How do changes in the value of the key explanatory variable translate into actual changes in policy? This invites horizontal comparisons, because it concerns the relationship between the key explanatory variable and the identified mechanisms, and is relevant for shedding light on the relationship between capital competitors' policies and the behavior of a given country. For this question, we would be particularly drawn to within-country cases in which there is a change in the capital competitors' variable over a number of years, and the country in question either adopted/did not adopt a liberal capital policy at any point. The within-country comparisons are also attractive because they help us to understand the temporal aspects of the diffusion process. By studying multiple within-case comparisons, we improve our ability to generate hypotheses about how the mechanisms function and their relationship to the key explanatory variable. In particular, we are drawn to France in the early 1990s, because its value for capital competitors' policy increased over time, as did our measure of expected relationships until 1994, when France adopted its liberal capital policy. Another case is South Korea, also during the 1990s. Between 1990 and 1994, there is an increase in the value of its capital competitors' variable, but South Korea did not adopt a liberal capital account policy.[6] Norway during the early 1990s is also a relevant case to study because it features a large expected relationship and it adopted a liberal capital policy in 1996. The full model gives Norway a much higher estimated probability of adopting a liberal capital policy in 1994, 1995, and 1996, but it is only in 1996 that Norway actually adopts its policy. For our purposes, studying Norway during these years would be useful in developing hypotheses about the conditions under which the key explanatory variable is associated with policy change. Selecting cases in which we can observe the same countries over time helps us understand the temporal aspects of policy diffusion, and studying multiple cases during the same time period would be useful for studying how policies spread between countries.

The second question that occurs is: What explains the variation in the outcomes among cases with similar expected relationships and values of the capital competitors' variable? This is a question that centers on vertical comparisons, and focusing on a question like this is

---

[6] This raises the possibility that some cases feature no or a negative relationship between changes in the capital competitors' variable, even though the average relationship suggests that increases in the explanatory variable are associated with a higher probability of the event occurring.

useful for investigating the number, direction, and possible interactions between mechanisms. For instance, clustered around six on the x-axis are countries that have quite similar expected relationships, and yet there is variation in whether or not the outcome occurred. This raises the prospect of trying to understand the number of mechanisms and their possible interactions. For example: Does the capital competitors' mechanism(s) act independently from other possible mechanisms? Or, is there some other mechanism(s) that either accentuates or suppresses the effect of the capital competitors' variable? These answers would help build knowledge about which of the scenarios from Table 2.1 in Chapter 2 best fit the research question.

The third question that occurs is: Why do the outcomes differ among countries with the most-common values of the policy of capital competitors' variable (between 1.6 and 2.2)? Understanding the different outcomes among the countries in this region is important because it may help us understand the relationship between the mechanism(s) and the outcome. For instance, it may be that the capital competitors' variable only affects policy outcomes in the presence of some other factors, and we may shed light on that via pathway analysis. This is akin to building knowledge about the conditions under which a particular pathway is likely to exist, and is crucial to a more complete understanding of how mechanisms function.

5.3 Case selection for measurement validity

Before ending our discussion on selecting cases regarding policy diffusion, it is useful to consider how to select cases that probe measurement validity, which is an important potential use of mixed-method research. To start, we turn again to Figure 5.3, which examines the estimated relationship between the capital competitors' variable and adoption of a liberal capital account policy. As we argued in Chapter 2, a good measure should identify both the presence and absence of the underlying concept. However, since we are only concerned with the validity of the independent variable, we do not pay attention to whether a country actually adopts a liberal capital policy or the estimated effect of the variable. Ensuring that cases are comparable is less important, because the task requires us to pick cases that feature variation in underlying measures. To this end, for our purposes, an ideal approach is a stratified random sample in which we stratify based on values of the relevant variable and then select randomly from within each strata. This approach has the following virtues:

- It ensures cases are selected from across the range of the independent variable.
- It ensures that a reasonable number of cases are chosen from each stratum of the possible levels of independent variable.
- It avoids selecting cases in which a researcher knows about the presence or absence of the key explanatory variable, because even if the measure is valid in a subset of cases, it does not help a researcher know if it is valid in other cases.

Any conclusions a researcher comes to about measurement validity are enhanced if the observed cases are representative of the unobserved cases. Although this is difficult with a small number of cases, the stratified random sampling approach can help a researcher be more confident in their selection of cases.

5.4   Conclusion

This chapter offers several core lessons. First, from the perspective of pathway analysis, the relevant empirical literature is often messy and not neatly organized into claims about explanatory variables, mechanisms, and outcomes. It is crucial for researchers to recognize this and to be prepared to interpret the existing literature in light of the broader purposes of a multi-method research agenda. In the context of our policy diffusion example, this entails looking past the labels used in the existing literature to see how different variables were actually used. Once a researcher realizes what is called a mechanism in the literature is, for purposes of pathway analysis, an explanatory variable in a longer causal chain, it is possible to apply our method and leverage the existing large-N data to select promising cases. Second, this chapter illustrates some practical tools for addressing temporal dynamics in selecting cases for pathway analysis, such as combining within-case comparisons with across-case comparisons that allows an investigation across both time and space. Finally, when there is an interest in using mixed-method research for probing measurement validity, moving from a purposive sampling strategy to a random stratified sample can be quite useful.

<table><tr><td>**6**</td><td></td></tr></table>

Matching to select cases for pathway analysis

<table><tr><td>**6.1**</td><td>**Introduction**</td></tr></table>

In the previous chapters, we used a regression-based approach for case selection. Like any approach, relying on regression has important trade-offs that researchers need to be aware of. Perhaps most importantly, this approach relies on the functional form assumptions of the underlying regression analysis, which researchers may not want to adopt in selecting cases for pathway analysis. The good news is that there is nothing about pathway analysis that *requires* the use of regression analysis. We have concentrated on regression analysis because it is well known by researchers, and we think likely to be used in practice. We recognize that there are a host of other options to leverage existing large-N data to select cases for comparative pathway analysis.[1]

This chapter illustrates one alternative to regression-based case selection. It explores how a researcher might use a common matching approach to select cases, and we apply the technique to an example we also discuss in the next chapter: the relationship between natural resource exports and civil conflict. A matching approach is useful, because it is explicitly designed for making comparisons. This is valuable in our context, because it fits well with the underlying importance

---

[1] We also anticipate that the options will continue to expand, as new techniques are developed, especially those aimed at better identifying unit level effects.

of comparative research strategies.[2] It is worth noting that others have also combined matching approaches with case studies, but the goal in prior approaches has been to understand causal effects (Nielsen 2014; Rosenbaum and Silber 2001); in general, matching approaches aimed at improving causal inference focus on identifying comparable treatment and control cases based on pretreatment co-variates that are related to treatment (Ho et al. 2007; Rubin 2008). In pathway analysis, however, the goal differs. By definition, pathway analysis assumes that the causal effect has been identified in previous scholarship and matching is used as a means to identify cases that are appropriate for exploring the mechanisms underlying the previously identified relationship.

As explained in more detail later in this chapter, a researcher can use a common matching approach to help identify outcome and non-outcome cases that are as similar as possible. Once pairs of comparable cases have been identified that differ in the outcome, it is possible to purposively sample which ones to study by using information about the similarity – or difference – in the co-variates, the outcome, and the key explanatory variable. To see how this works in practice, the remainder of this chapter works through the general steps for selecting cases, which by now should be familiar:

(1) assess if the requisites of pathway analysis are met;
(2) review the existing literature;
(3) visualize the data; and
(4) select the cases.

---

[2] Whether to use matching or regression-based approaches is not a clear-cut decision for most empirical research. This is also true in the context of pathway analysis: there will not be one approach that dominates. One reason the decision is not apparent is that the two methods are typically evaluated on their ability to recover causal effects, which is not our purpose here. Another reason, as Joshua Angrist and Jorn-Steffen Pischke (2009) make clear, is that regression is itself a form of matching, and the two methods may perform similarly when the goal is to understand causal effects.

In most ways, these steps will be the same as discussed in previous chapters. The key difference is that we use matching to implement steps 3 and 4. It should be stressed that this chapter is not intended as an exhaustive treatment of the many possible alternatives to regression-based case selection. It does, however, illustrate a promising alternative. It also serves as a useful reminder that researchers can be creative when leveraging existing large-N data to select cases for comparative pathway analysis.

6.2   Step 1: Assess if the requisites of pathway analysis are met

The first step in our approach is to assess whether the relevant literature establishes a robust relationship between levels of primary exports (X1) and civil war (Y), and if it provides the data needed to apply this approach. The short answer is that the literature meets these threshold criteria, but several points are worth noting about the X1/Y relationship at this stage of the process. In the original Paul Collier and Anke Hoeffler (2004) article, the authors focus on the onset of civil conflict and how it relates to the level of primary exports in a country. In their regression analysis, Collier and Hoeffler include both a country's level of primary exports and its square as the key explanatory variables in predicting the onset of civil conflict, and they find that both are significantly related to the probability of civil conflict. More specifically, the level of primary exports is positively related to the onset of conflict and the squared level of primary exports is negatively related. The negative coefficient on the squared level of primary commodities indicates that beyond a certain level of primary exports, exports are associated with a reduction in the probability of civil war. Overall, this creates an inverted U-shaped relationship between primary exports and probability of civil war. As we discuss below, understanding this aspect of the functional form is important in deciding which cases to study and the types of questions to explore.

6.3 Step 2: Review the existing literature

Once a researcher decides the preconditions for pathway analysis have been met, the next step is to review the existing literature to understand how the research fits with and contributes to prior knowledge. The main purpose of this step is to determine the type of knowledge that will hopefully be gained from the case studies. As seen in Chapter 5, this requires a careful reading of the literature. For our purposes, we focus on Michael Ross' 2004 article, because he is a leading expert on the topic and in this article he conducts a sophisticated pathway analysis in this area of study. According to Ross (2004), knowledge about the mechanisms connecting primary resource experts and civil war is fairly limited. He identifies four commonly mentioned mechanisms: looting, grievances, incentives for separatism, and state weakness. Ross uses his case studies partly to search for the possibility of new mechanisms. In doing so, he identifies two new possible mechanisms: sale of future rights to primary exports and intervention from a third party. Overall this suggests there may be as many as six mechanisms; however, we do not know if this is an exhaustive list or if these mechanisms might interact with each other. To use the language from Chapter 2, we know that scenarios 1 and 2 do not apply because there are multiple mechanisms, but we cannot be sure how many mechanisms there are, or if these mechanisms are exclusive (scenario 3, Multiple Exclusive Pathways) or interactive (scenario 4, Multiple Non-Exclusive Pathways).

The primary task of pathway analysis then is to gain insights into the basic underlying relationships among the key explanatory variable, mechanisms, and outcome. Given this goal, initial questions for pathway analysis are: (1) whether the mechanisms are, in fact, the only mechanisms that connect primary exports and civil conflict, and (2) whether the mechanisms occur independently of each other. If the mechanisms are not independent, then we might be able to improve our understanding of which mechanisms occur together and how often or likely they are to occur at the same time. This is crucial information for understanding the substantive relationship between primary exports and civil conflict, because it helps us to understand whether any of these mechanisms are independent of each other and the conditions under which reliance on primary exports is associated with civil conflict.

6.4   Step 3: Visualize key variation

With this background in mind, we can visualize variation within the large-N data. In some ways, this process will be very familiar: the two criteria that guide case selection are the expected relationship between X1/Y and variation in case characteristics. As in earlier chapters, we start by visualizing the distribution of the X1 variable and then turn to the expected relationship between X1 and Y. The difference is that, in this chapter, visualizing the expected relationship is based on a matching approach, not regression estimates.

6.4.1   A distributional plot of primary exports

We begin by examining the distribution of the key explanatory variable – primary exports as a percentage of a country's GDP – to help us get a sense of how common different values of this variable are in the data.

The histogram makes it clear that the vast bulk of countries have relatively low levels of primary exports (see Figure 6.1). Therefore, for the purpose of picking cases that have common values of the primary exports variable, we focus on cases with values below 0.2 of primary exports, because more than 70 percent of cases have levels of primary exports/GDP that are at or below this level. Among the 46 countries in the Collier and Hoeffler dataset that experienced a civil war, the average level of primary exports/GDP was 0.15; the 25th percentile was 0.07; and the 75th percentile was 0.20. This is a useful initial step regardless of the approach used to analyze the large-N data, because knowledge

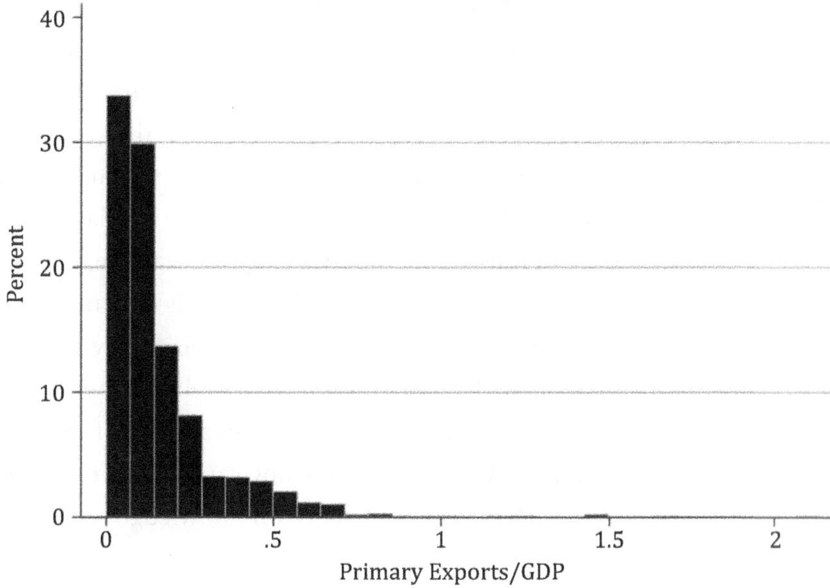

Figure 6.1   Distribution of primary exports

of the distribution of the key explanatory variable helps us to understand how the cases we eventually study relate to the cases we do not study.

6.4.2   Estimate and visualize the expected X1/Y relationship

The second piece of information we utilize in the case selection process is our estimate of the expected relationship between X1 and Y. Here, we utilize a matching approach to understand the expected X1/Y relationship. The basic intuition is to identify cases that differ in their outcome and in the value of the key explanatory variable, but that are as similar as possible based on co-variates other than the key explanatory variable(s). We use knowledge of the outcome in the case selection process, which differs from the standard advice about both case selection and matching (see King et al. 1994; Rubin 2008). In pathway analysis we are not concerned with casual inference, but instead are trying to learn about the pathways that connect X1 to Y, and for that reason some of the standard guidelines for both case selection and matching do not apply.

The matching approach we present in this chapter uses the Mahalanobis distance to identify the distance (or the similarity) between cases based on the observed values of variables selected by a researcher. (For a review of different ways to measure the similarity between cases, see Stuart and Rubin 2007.) Researchers identify the relevant set of variables from which to compute the Mahalanobis distance, and these variables should ideally occur before the key explanatory variable and represent factors that make the cases comparable. It is important that the variables used for matching are not themselves a result of the treatment. There is no formulaic approach to choosing variables from which to compute the distance metric, rather it relies on knowledge of a particular empirical and theoretical literature.

The use of the Mahalanobis distance is a flexible approach to matching that allows for the identification of ideal matches for each case of interest (discussed later in this chapter). For our application, we use the Mahalanobis distance both to identify the ideal matches for each outcome case and to determine the distance between the matched cases on the key explanatory variable. Based on these two distance measures, we can select cases based on their similarity/difference on the chosen matching variables and the key explanatory variable.

It is worth stressing that although specific techniques of large-N analysis differ, the *comparative* logic of the underlying exercise remains the same regardless of whether one is using matching or regression. So, for example, all things being equal, in probing the basic X1/Y relationship, it would be interesting to identify cases where X1 and X2 are similar but the outcomes differ, or cases where X2 and the outcome are the same but X1 differs.

To work through the example, we need to take a closer look at the dataset we use in this chapter, which is from Collier and Hoeffler (2004). The first thing we note is that these data feature a dichotomous outcome. This allows us to implement a standard bipartite matching technique (i.e., cases are either in the outcome/treatment or in the non-outcome/non-treatment groups).[3] In this dataset, countries are observed every seven years, and each country can appear at most five possible times. In the data we use there are a total of 688 observations and 46 observations (five-year periods for a country) feature the beginning of a civil conflict.

To estimate the expected relationship between civil conflict and natural resources using these data, we begin with each of the 46 cases in which the outcome (civil conflict) occurred. We then use the co-variates, other than the key explanatory variables, identified by Collier and Hoeffler to compute the Mahalanobis distance between each outcome case and each non-outcome case.[4] For each outcome case we then select the non-outcome case with the smallest distance as the ideal match for that case.[5] In this matching process we treat each observation in the dataset as a separate observation and do not place any restrictions on which cases are matched to the outcome cases, other than that it must be a non-outcome case. Therefore, it is possible that a particular non-war case will be the closest match for multiple war cases. In addition, the approach may identify possible within-case comparisons (i.e., matching Iran 1980 to Iran 1985) or cross-case comparisons (i.e., matching Iran 1980 to Algeria 1970). For each matched pair of cases we also compute a Mahalanobis distance based on the level of primary exports and the squared value

---

[3] There are matching techniques for non-bipartite situations in which the variable that determines treated/untreated or outcome/non-outcome is not dichotomous (Lu et al. 2011), but they are less commonly used. In addition, the application of non-bipartite matching is for situations that feature multiple levels of a treatment variable (i.e., a categorical or ordinal measure), not for scenarios with a truly continuous variable.

[4] All of the Mahalanobis distances are computed in STATA 12 using the MAHAPICK package (Kantor 2006).

[5] The variables used to compute the Mahalanobis distance for matching non-outcome and outcome cases are: post-Cold War period, male enrollment in secondary education, GDP growth, duration of peace, existence of a prior conflict, presence of mountainous terrain, geographic dispersion, social fractionalization, and log of total population.

of the level of primary exports, which are the key explanatory variables studied by Collier and Hoeffler (2004). Overall this provides us with two useful pieces of information for each match between an outcome and non-outcome case: the overall distance between the cases based on the co-variates used to identify comparable cases and the distance between the two cases on the key explanatory variable.

In Table 6.1, we list each outcome case and its matched non-outcome case, as well as the overall distance between the cases and the distance between the cases on the key explanatory variables (primary exports/GDP and its square). Although for each outcome case we identify the case that is closest in terms of Mahalanobis distance, there is still significant variation in how close any pair of cases is to each other. In addition, among the matched pairs there is great variation in how similar they are on the primary exports variable. As we discuss in the next section, this variation in distance between cases can be useful in selecting cases for pathway analysis. Upon perusing the list of cases in Table 6.1, it is immediately obvious that this approach to matching identifies numerous within-country pairs of cases, in which the closest match was the same country in a different time period.

We then construct a scatterplot (see Figure 6.2) to help us visualize variation in the distance between the cases based on the two different Mahalanobis distances. Each point on the scatterplot represents a matched pair of war and non-war cases: the x-axis captures the distance between each pair on the variables used to identify the match, and the y-axis represents the distance between the cases on the key explanatory variable. We labeled each observation with the level of primary exports for the outcome (war) cases, because this can be used in conjunction with Figure 6.1 to shed light on how the value of primary exports compares to the overall sample of cases. Figure 6.2, therefore, allows us to visualize how each pair of matched cases compares to the other pairs of matched cases.

Unlike regression-based approaches to case selection, we do not provide an explicit formula for the expected X1/Y relationship. Rather

Table 6.1 Matched pairs of war and non-war cases

War case	Non-war case	Distance: based on co-variates	Distance: based on primary exports
Colombia 1980	Argentina 1970	0.3193	0.1548
Morocco 1975	Morocco 1970	0.4506	0.1015
Philippines 1970	Philippines 1965	0.4580	0.0448
India 1980	India 1975	0.4675	0.0059
Nicaragua 1975	Nicaragua 1970	0.4678	0.0055
Burundi 1985	Rwanda 1975	0.4891	0.0172
Somalia 1980	Somalia 1975	0.4961	0.5553
Congo 1995	Congo 1990	0.5231	0.0003
Sierra Leone 1990	Central African Republic 1990	0.5593	0.2186
Sudan 1980	Sudan 1975	0.6222	0.0108
El Salvador 1975	El Salvador 1970	0.6389	0.1468
Indonesia 1975	Indonesia 1970	0.6523	0.7411
Sri Lanka 1970	Sri Lanka 1965	0.9722	0.3630
Zimbabwe 1970	Zimbabwe 1965	0.9807	0.6788
Pakistan 1970	Mexico 1970	0.9900	0.0074
Ethiopia 1970	Ethiopia 1965	1.1377	0.0531
India 1965	India 1975	1.1657	0.0093
Uganda 1965	Ghana 1965	1.1771	0.0205
Angola 1990	Mozambique 1995	1.2238	5.6942
Uganda 1980	Uganda 1975	1.2587	1.4623
Sri Lanka 1980	Sri Lanka 1975	1.3262	0.3860
Dominican Republic 1965	Saudi Arabia 1970	1.3640	8.3128
Iran 1975	Iran 1985	1.3717	5.1692
Peru 1980	Chile 1985	1.5984	0.3425
Myanmar/Burma 1980	Pakistan 1980	1.6113	0.0393
Iraq 1970	Tunisia 1965	1.7459	1.2106
Mozambique 1975	Sudan 1975	1.8557	0.0001
Iran 1970	Iran 1965	1.8792	0.0000
Romania 1985	Romania 1980	1.9228	0.0595
Guatemala 1965	Bolivia 1965	2.2501	0.1848
Nigeria 1980	Zaire 1975	2.3007	2.2785
Turkey 1990	Nepal 1990	2.3690	0.1141
Algeria 1990	Argentina 1990	2.4892	0.9426

(*cont.*)

Table 6.1 (*cont.*)

War case	Non-war case	Distance: based on co-variates	Distance: based on primary exports
Guatemala 1975	Guatemala 1985	2.8736	0.1737
Myanmar/Burma 1965	Philippines 1965	3.1561	0.0267
Somalia 1985	Zimbabwe 1980	3.2960	0.2384
Burundi 1970	Burundi 1965	3.4863	0.0305
Nigeria 1965	Ghana 1965	3.7900	0.0150
Nicaragua 1980	Guatemala 1985	4.3039	0.5053
Angola 1975	Guatemala 1985	4.4471	3.9430
Zaire 1990	Ivory Coast 1995	5.0134	5.7690
Burundi 1990	Guatemala 1990	5.9325	0.1971
Zaire 1995	Nigeria 1990	6.0230	2.5502
Rwanda 1990	Lesotho 1990	7.6490	0.0514
Iraq 1985	Dominican Republic 1985	8.3061	0.4477
Iran 1980	Guatemala 1985	8.8363	0.2480

in this matching approach we assume the expected X1/Y relationship is greatest (and therefore our ability to identify causal mechanisms is maximized) when a pair of cases are very similar (small Mahalanobis distance) overall, but differ significantly in the distance computed from the key explanatory variable(s). For instance, in Figure 6.2, we expect that case pairs near the upper left of the scatterplot provide the comparisons that are most promising for identifying mechanisms that connect primary exports to civil conflict. By selecting multiple pairs of cases, it is possible for us to explore questions related to the number of possible mechanisms (or at least a lower bound estimate) and how they might interact. We should note that the information in Figure 6.2 may not be sufficient to identify the cases to select. Rather, we might want to combine the information in Figure 6.2 with information about the actual values of the key explanatory variables, because that might help us to combine the information in Figure 6.2 with the histogram in Figure 6.1.

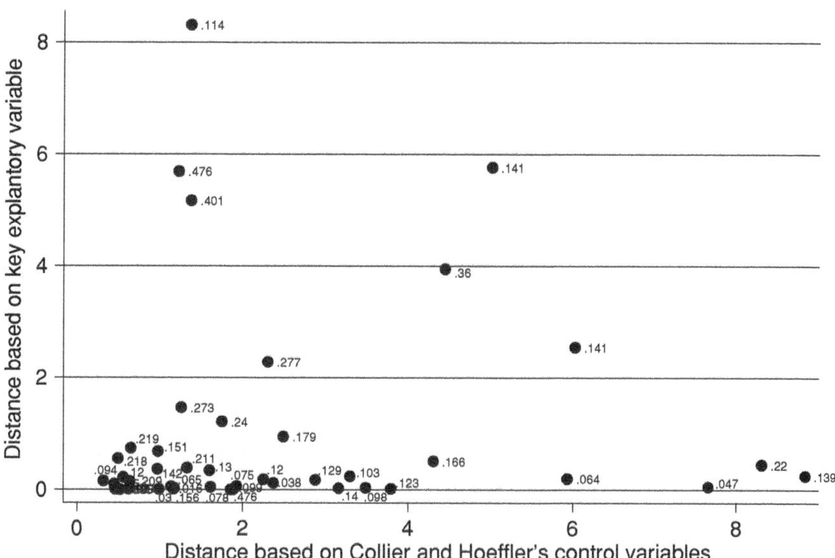

Figure 6.2   Scatterplot of Mahalanobis distances for matched pairs of cases

6.5   Select the cases

The final step is to select cases in light of the available data and goals of a research agenda and pathway analysis. We previously suggested that researchers think vertically and horizontally to identify interesting patterns of variation in cases. Therefore, we return to Figure 6.2 to look for these types of comparisons. It is worthwhile to remember that in this figure each point represents a matched pair of cases and, therefore, we ultimately select multiple pairs of cases for pathway analysis.

In terms of vertical patterns of cases, there are pairs of cases near zero on the x-axis (these are the most similar pairs) that vary quite substantially in how similar they are in terms of the key explanatory variable (on the y-axis). The pairs of cases in this region (upper left of Figure 6.2) represent the closest match based on the Mahalanobis distance computed from all non-explanatory variables, but the cases differ in outcome and may differ in the Mahalanobis distance computed from the explanatory variables. Pairs of cases that differ in explanatory variable and outcome, but that are similar based on the distance measure, provide the most promising cases to observe the causal mechanisms that connect X1 to Y. The reason is that in these pairs of cases, we can be most confident that it is the X1 variable that differs between the two cases and therefore it should be associated with mechanisms that lead to the difference in outcome. Studying pairs of cases such as these provides an opportunity to study how many mechanisms might exist and perhaps whether such mechanisms interact. This type of information can help ascertain whether mechanisms are mutually exclusive.

Based on this idea, it would be instructive to pick one of the matched pairs of cases at the top-left side of Figure 6.2. The pair of cases with the greatest distance in the key explanatory variable is the Dominican Republic in 1965 and Saudi Arabia in 1970. At first glance this may seem an odd case from the perspective of an expected relationship, because although the two differ substantially in the value of primary exports/GDP, the non-war case (Saudi Arabia) has a much greater level of primary exports/GDP. Keep in mind, however, that there is a curvilinear relationship between primary exports and the probability of conflict. Therefore, even though the cases have quite different levels of primary exports, the relationship between primary exports and conflict might be quite similar. Studying these two cases might help shed light on why low and high levels of primary exports are associated with similar probabilities of conflict. Do some mechanisms have a positive effect and others a negative effect on civil conflict? And does the mix of mechanisms vary with the level of primary exports?

In terms of a large expected relationship between X1 and Y, another pair of cases is more appropriate: in particular, comparing Iran in 1975 (war case) to Iran 1985 (non-war case). This comparison has the added advantage of being a within-case comparison, which helps to account for differences between the cases not captured by the matching variables. By studying these two cases we provided ourselves with a good chance to observe the mechanisms that connect primary exports to civil conflict by looking for mechanisms that are absent in one case but present in the other.

Other possible comparisons, based on vertical differences, are cases that are close in the distance computed from both the explanatory variable and the other co-variates, but still have different outcomes (these cases are in the lower left of Figure 6.2). The point in using such comparisons is to see if we can identify different mechanisms. If we did, how are mechanisms different and could we identify any hypotheses about why cases that are similar in both co-variates and explanatory variable have different mechanisms and outcomes? Is there a mechanism that inhibits the effect of primary exports?

We encourage researchers to think horizontally in their case selection, as well. In this example, that means looking at matched pairs of cases that are similar in distance, based on the explanatory variable, but that differ in the Mahalanobis distance calculated from the other co-variates. These cases are generally near the x-axis and stretch from left to right in Figure 6.2. The pairs of cases at the far lower right of Figure 6.2 are similar in terms of the key explanatory variable, but different in terms of both the outcome and the distance measure computed from the co-variates identified by Collier and Hoeffler. These pairs of cases still represent the best possible match for a given outcome case, but the distance between the two cases is relatively large compared to the other matched pairs of cases. Researchers might choose to study Rwanda 1990 (war case) and Lesotho 1990 (non-war case), because these two cases differ in the outcome, are quite close in distance based on the explanatory variable, and are relatively far apart in overall distance. Meanwhile, pairs of cases from the lower right area shed light on a variety of important questions. For instance: Do the mechanisms differ in the two cases? If so, do the mechanisms depend on identifiable differences between the cases? If yes, can we develop a hypothesis about how such differences might lead to different outcomes even when the key explanatory variables are similar?

As in prior chapters, there is no mechanical approach to the actual selection of cases to study. Rather, researchers will want to use the results of the matching procedure to help them pick cases given their particular research question and logistical constraints. The matching approach, however, provides an empirical, data-based technique for identifying promising candidates for comparative pathway analysis.[6]

6.6   Conclusion

In this chapter we demonstrated how researchers can use a matching-based approach to select cases for comparative pathway analysis. The matching approach we use has two primary benefits. First, it does not rely on functional form assumptions, although it does still rely on researchers having the appropriate data and knowledge to generate good matches between outcome and non-outcome cases. Second, a matching-based approach directly produces cases for comparative analysis. In fact, the entire rationale for matching is to identify comparable cases (or groups of cases) for analysis. Given that comparative analysis is critical to our approach, we see this as a benefit. However, it should be noted that the matching approach does not provide an individual-level estimate of the expected relationship between X1 and Y, as happens in the regression-based approach. As a result, the matching-based approach does not give the researcher as much flexibility in choosing which cases to compare, because the matching approach identifies the outcome and non-outcome cases to use as a comparison. Researchers will have to decide how many and which pairs of cases to select for comparative analysis of pathways.

The broader theme of this chapter is that our approach should not be applied mechanically. In seeking to select cases for comparative analysis of pathways, the critical goal is to select cases that vary across the

---

[6] There are other possible ways to estimate the expected relationship between X1 and Y, using either regression- or non-regression-based methods. We discuss a number of additional ways in documents available on our website at dornsife.usc.edu/weller.

expected relationship between X1/Y and key case characteristics. In seeking to satisfy these criteria, researchers need to leverage existing theory, empirical knowledge, and large-N data. Using regression analysis or other techniques, such as matching, can do this. The important point is that the various steps of our approach are flexible enough to accommodate different case selection techniques, remembering that the goal is to identify promising cases for comparing how X1 affects Y.

Using large-*N* methods to gain perspective on prior case studies

Introduction

So far in this book we have focused on using various quantitative methods to guide case selection in order to explore the substantive relationship between a key explanatory variable (X1) and an outcome (Y). The discussion assumes that, in some settings, researchers do not have strong reasons for selecting particular cases, and so are using quantitative data to determine case selection. However, in other cases, researchers often have compelling reasons for examining certain cases, including theoretical, empirical, and practical reasons (such as access to data sources, cost effectiveness, and preexisting expertise). Under these circumstances, the issue is not which cases to choose initially, but how to gain perspective on the cases already chosen and perhaps how to choose cases for additional analysis.

This chapter illustrates how large-N data can help gain perspective on previously chosen cases by shedding light on how they fit within the broader universe of cases that could have been chosen, thus providing some leverage over how the extant case studies compare to unstudied cases. This can help a researcher understand how to generalize to unstudied cases and how to identify future cases that might offer promising comparisons.

The use of large-N data to gain perspective on previously selected cases is best explored by example. In this chapter we focus on the relationship between natural resources (X1) and civil conflict (Y), which was also the focus of Chapter 6. We first explain why this example is useful, then we review the existing pathway analyses conducted by Michael Ross (2004) and the large-N data analysis of Paul Collier and Anke Hoeffler (2004), and finally we demonstrate how to use the large-N data to gain some perspective on the cases selected by Ross and how to identify avenues for future inquiry.

7.2   Natural resources and civil conflict

We focus on the relationship between natural resources and civil conflict because it is important substantively and because there are widely cited examples of both large-N (Collier and Hoeffler 2004) and small-N (Ross 2004) research related to how a country's primary exports (as a percentage of GDP) affect civil war. Collier and Hoeffler (2004) use large-N methods to explore the relationship between primary exports and civil war. Their article has been cited more than 3,000 times on Google Scholar, suggesting that theirs is an influential argument. The presence of a relationship between primary exports and conflict has led several researchers to propose different causal mechanisms that might underlie the primary export–civil war relationship, which Ross (2004) investigates via a number of case studies that he selected based on the secondary literature, without use of Collier and Hoeffler's large-N data. As such, his studies offer a good opportunity to illustrate how large-N data might contextualize cases studied in a small-N analysis. It should be stressed that our goal is not to critique Ross' findings, nor is there reason to believe that his findings are incorrect. Rather, our goal is to show how large-N data can be used to provide some perspective on previously studied cases, and therefore help to interpret the results and perhaps to consider how to build on the existing research.

7.3   Pathway analysis of primary exports and civil conflict

Researchers in this field have engaged in small-N research to tease out the mechanisms that link primary exports to civil conflict. In his ambitious study, Ross (2004) conducts 13 case studies to investigate the causal mechanisms purported to underlie this link. Although Ross did not call his research pathway analysis, he was clearly engaged in what we consider pathway analysis because he focused on exploring causal mechanisms across a number of cases in order to shed light on this important substantive research question. Ross was appropriately aware of the limits of his case studies. He recognized that he could not identify average effects or definitively demonstrate or rule out particular mechanisms using his research design, but his goal was to determine if there was evidence for the existence of a purported causal mechanism and endeavored to identify new mechanisms if they existed. In the language of Chapter 2, Ross was uncertain about which scenario applied and was using pathway analysis to probe the basic structure of the X1/Y relationship, especially the number and identity of the key mechanisms linking natural resource wealth and civil conflict.

Ross considered a variety of different mechanisms that relate to the onset, duration, or intensity of civil war. In this chapter we focus on the mechanisms he identified that are related to the onset of conflict, because this is the relationship explored by Collier and Hoeffler (2004) in their large-*N* study of civil conflict, which we use in the next section to help contextualize Ross' cases. Ross initially identifies four mechanisms that could connect primary export levels to civil conflict: looting by potential rebels, grievances among locals, incentives for separatism, and state weakness due to reliance on revenue from natural resource. To see if the hypothesized mechanisms actually existed, Ross selected 13 "most likely" cases, which he defined as a civil war having occurred and in which his reading of secondary source material suggested that primary exports played a role in the origin of the conflict. It is unclear if "most likely" means that observing the relationship is most likely, if observing a particular mechanism is most likely, or if it means something different altogether. Regardless, Ross' case selection process was (like ours) clearly designed to use some observable indicators to pick cases that he then examined to study whether as-yet-unobserved causal mechanisms were present. In Table 7.1, we list the 13 cases Ross studied as well as

Table 7.1 Case-by-case results from Ross' case studies

Country	Looting	Grievance	Separatism	Other
Congo Republic	No	No	–	Yes
Angola	No	No	–	No
Liberia	No	No	–	No
Indonesia	No	–	Yes	No
Congo, Democratic Republic, I	No	No	–	No
Congo, Democratic Republic, II	No	No	–	Yes
Peru	No	No	–	No
Sierra Leone	No	No	–	Yes
Colombia	No	No	–	No
Sudan	No	–	Yes	No
Myanmar/Burma	No	–	No	No
Cambodia	No	No	–	No
Afghanistan	No	No	–	No

Source: Ross (2004: 50).

his conclusions regarding the presence of a particular mechanism that connects primary resources to civil conflict.

In general, Ross found little support for the purported mechanisms but did identify two unanticipated mechanisms: "sale of future rights to war booty" and intervention from a third party (Ross 2004: 50). Overall he argued that there was "no evidence in the sample of the looting mechanism, and little if any evidence of the grievance mechanism" (50). This only pertained to the 13 cases in Ross' sample, and therefore any general conclusions a researcher might draw depend crucially on how these cases compare to the many unstudied cases. Put differently, it is necessary to gain some perspective on Ross' cases.

7.4   The large-*N* data

In seeking perspective on preexisting research, we encourage researchers to use the same basic tools as when selecting cases; only now the goal is to understand how the already chosen cases fit into the distribution of

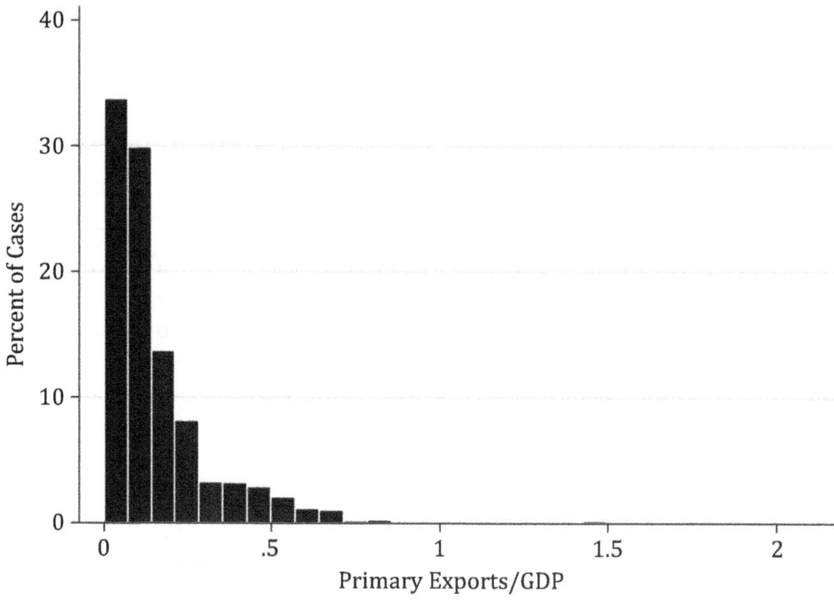

Figure 7.1   Distribution of primary exports variable

X1 values and expected relationships. We refer to the data from Collier and Hoeffler (2004) in this section to do this. In the Collier and Hoeffler dataset, each observation is a country–time period, and the time period is five years. The original data range from 1960 to 1995, so an individual country can appear at most seven times in the dataset. There are 46 cases in which there was a civil conflict in a country during a five-year time period. We first present the relevant results from Collier and Hoeffler's large-*N* data and then use this data to shed light on Ross' selected cases.

The first step examines the distribution of the primary exports variable in the histogram in Figure 7.1.[1] It becomes immediately obvious that the vast bulk of cases have very few primary exports, and therefore a researcher must be aware of this when selecting cases, because

---

[1] Ross refers to this variable as primary exports/GDP, while Collier and Hoeffler referred to it as primary commodities/GDP. We use Ross' terminology.

Table 7.2 Relationship between primary exports and civil conflict

	Full model	Reduced model
Primary exports	18.1 (6.00)**	–
Primary exports squared	–27.44 (11.22)*	–
Post-Cold War period	–0.32 (0.47)	–0.33 (0.45)
Male enrollment, secondary education	–0.025 (0.01)*	–0.019 (0.009)*
GDP growth	–0.12 (0.04)**	–0.13 (0.04)**
Peace duration	–0.0025 (0.0016)	–0.002 (0.01)
Previous war	–.46 (0.54)	0.69 (0.52)
Mountainous terrain	0.013 (0.009)	0.006 (0.008)
Geographic dispersion	–2.21 (1.03)*	–1.40 (0.98)
Social fractionalization	–0.0001 (0.00009)	–0.00006 (0.00009)
Log of population	0.67 (0.16)**	0.37 (0.12)
Constant	–12.33 (2.71)**	–6.56 (1.94)**
N	688	688
Number of wars	46	46

Note: * = significant at 0.05 level; ** = significant at 0.01 level. Results in Reduced model column (column 2) restricted to the same set of observations used in Full model column (column 1); eight observations are excluded from column 2 by restricting the observations to be consistent with column 1.

high levels of primary commodities are uncommon in the data and it is possible that the mechanisms in those cases are anomalous.

Once we have a sense of the distribution of primary exports (X1), the next step is to examine the expected relationship between primary exports and civil war (Y) for the cases chosen by Ross. To do this, we compute the predicted probability of a civil war (Y) with and without the primary exports variable (X1) using a logit regression. There are certainly other ways one can estimate a case-level expected relationship, but our aim in this chapter is to demonstrate how to use existing quantitative studies to contextualize cases. Therefore, in Table 7.2, we present the exact regression from Collier and Hoeffler in column 1 and a reduced form of the same equation that excludes the primary exports variables in column 2 (similar to what we did in Chapter 5). An important note for case selection is that the large-*N* regression included both the primary exports variable and its square. The implication of this is that the effect of additional primary exports begins to decline at some point and the overall relationship between primary exports levels and probability of civil conflict will resemble an inverted-U. Using the two regressions from Table 7.2, we computed the predicted probability of a war including the primary exports variable and the predicted probability of a war without this variable. We subtract the predicted probability based on the reduced model from the full model, and this difference is the measure of the expected relationship. If the predicted probability is higher in the model that includes the natural resources variable then the expected relationship is positive, whereas if the predicted probability is higher in the reduced model, then the expected relationship is negative. Some cases had a positive expected relationship even though a war did not occur in that case.

We combined the measure of expected relationship with information about the values of X1 and Y to provide a better sense of how the cases Ross studied compare to the unstudied cases. A scatterplot with this information provides a useful way to contextualize cases. In Figure 7.2, the y-axis is our measure of expected relationship: the difference in the predicted probability between the model with primary exports and the model without primary exports. A positive number indicates that the predicted probability of conflict is higher in the model that includes the primary exports variable than in the model that excludes that variable. The x-axis is the value of the key independent variable: primary exports/GDP. Figure 7.2 also includes information about Y: did war occur or not. The "war" cases are marked with Xs, whereas the "non-war" cases are marked with 0s. In addition, the cases studied by Ross, for which the Collier and Hoeffler dataset has complete data, are labeled in Figure 7.2.

Although we believe the approach to contextualizing cases as represented by Figure 7.2 is superior when it is applicable, Ross studied a few cases for which missing data precluded our ability to compare predicted probabilities, as in Figure 7.2. Another way to estimate the

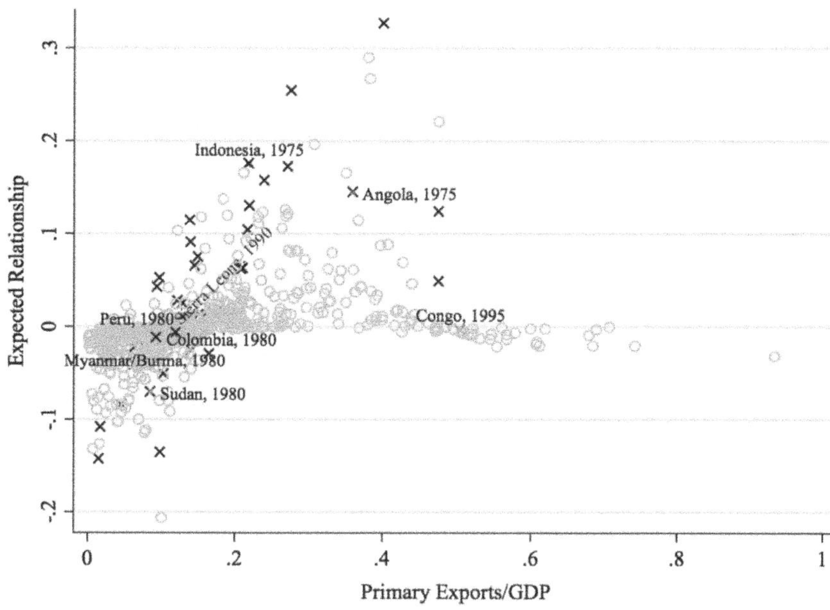

Note : ○ = non-war case   × = war case

Figure 7.2   Expected relationship and levels of primary exports

expected relationship for such cases is to plot the estimated change in the Y value (probability of civil conflict) at various values of the independent variable (primary exports). The relationship is not constant across values of primary exports (both because of the logit functional form and the squared term of primary exports); therefore we had to evaluate the marginal effect at different values of primary exports. One might use a figure such as this to get a sense of the expected relationship for cases where the value of primary exports is known. However, in this instance, some of the other data for the case were missing and so the case was not included in the regression, which eliminated directly comparing predicted probabilities. In Figure 7.3, we present the estimated marginal relationship between primary exports and the probability of civil conflict, holding the value of other variables at their means.[2]

---

[2] In a logit regression the estimated marginal effects depend on both the value of the primary explanatory variable and the additional control variables. Therefore, we had

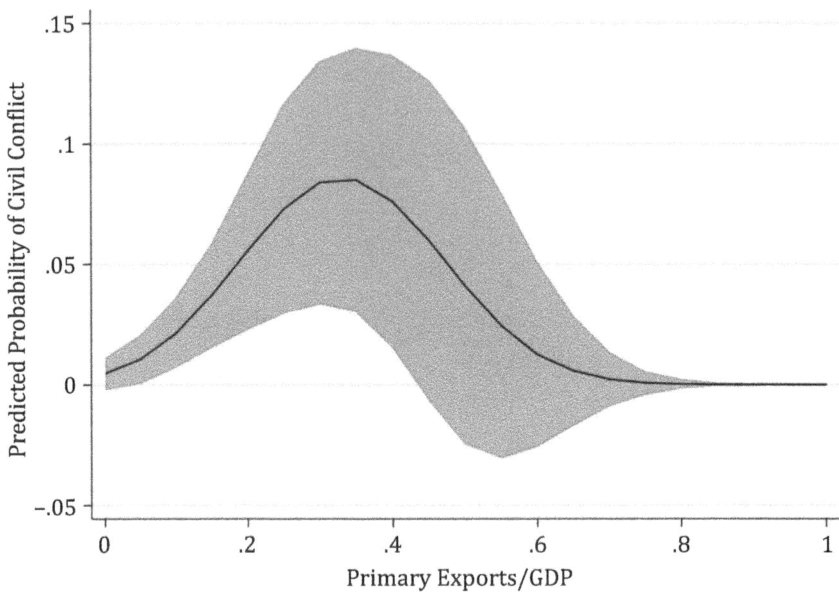

Figure 7.3   Marginal effect of primary exports on probability of civil war

Figure 7.3 demonstrates the expected inverted-U relationship between the level of primary exports and the probability of civil conflict and underscores the importance of understanding functional form in selecting cases. One implication from this curve is that choosing a critical case based on an extreme value of the primary resource variable would be a mistake, because beyond a primary exports value of about 0.4, higher values of primary resource dependence are associated with a lower probability of conflict. Figure 7.3 also shows that at the most extreme values of primary exports, there is little relationship between that and the likelihood of conflict. Another implication from the plot is that a one-unit change in primary exports has its largest relationship with

to decide which values to use for these additional variables. In this case, the estimated marginal effects (and the shape of the curve) were substantively similar if we held other variables at their median, 25th, or 75th percentile. This is a good thing for choosing cases because it suggests that our results are not highly sensitive to the value of other variables.

the probability of conflict in cases with intermediate values of primary exports – between 0.2 and 0.4, with the peak being just below 0.4.

7.5   Contextualizing Ross' case selection

Having visualized the Collier and Hoeffler data and having gained some familiarity with their analysis, we use the data to provide perspective on the cases Ross studies. The point is not to disagree with the conclusions Ross reaches in any given case. Indeed, Ross' pathway analysis is in many ways exemplary, especially in his careful interpretation of findings and his contribution to an understanding of the number of mechanisms connecting primary exports and civil war. Our goal is to understand how the cases he selects compare to all the other unselected cases.

Table 7.3 lists the cases Ross chooses in his case studies, as well as each case's value on the key explanatory variable, each case's expected relationship from the logit regression, and the estimated marginal effect based on each case's value of the primary export variable. A few things jump out regarding the context of these cases. First, in terms of the values of the primary export variable, the cases Ross chooses span much of the range of this key explanatory variable. Second, in most of these cases, the inclusion of the primary exports variable barely increases the predicted probability of a civil conflict. In fact, for a number of the cases the inclusion of primary exports appears to have *lowered* the predicted probability of a war. In his analysis of these 13 cases, Ross finds very limited support for the existing purported causal mechanisms. However, this may not be a surprise, given that these cases have relatively small change in predicted probability with the inclusion of primary exports. Third, in the few cases where we could not directly compute the expected relationship, the marginal effects approach suggests a small relationship between primary exports and civil conflict. Again, this implies that it might have been difficult to actually observe a causal mechanism in these cases.

Table 7.3 Cases chosen to study primary exports and civil conflict

Country	Year in Collier and Hoeffler data	Primary export/ GDP	Expected relationship	Marginal effect of primary exports
Congo Republic	1995	0.505	−0.003	0.04
Angola	1975	0.476	0.14	0.059
Liberia	1990	0.393	0.	0.076
Indonesia	1975	0.219	0.017	0.055
Congo, Democratic Republic	1995	0.141	–	0.037
Peru	1980	0.130	0.008	0.037
Sierra Leone	1990	0.120	−0.007	0.021
Colombia	1980	0.094	−0.013	0.021
Sudan	1980	0.086	−0.07	0.021
Myanmar/Burma	1980	0.078	−0.017	0.01
Cambodia	1970	0.052	–	0.01
Afghanistan	1990	0.033	–	0.01

Note: Cases based on Ross (2004). Marginal effects were estimated from the regression in column 1, Table 7.2 at every 0.05, from 0.00 to 0.50, and the listed effect corresponds to the estimated effect at the nearest level of primary exports with other variables held at their means.
Source: Ross (2004).

In addition to the expected relationship, it is important to consider how the chosen cases support generalizations to other, unobserved cases. Much to his credit, Ross is keenly aware of problems with making claims about other cases, explicitly stating: "[T]he findings cannot be generalized to some larger set of unexamined cases" (Ross 2004: 37). Although we agree that generalization can be difficult, a researcher's ability to make general claims about mechanisms will improve if cases are chosen that vary on important dimensions. It will also improve if a researcher adopts an explicitly comparative research strategy that allows observation of how mechanisms function across a wide range of relationships between X1 and Y, while also considering the distribution of X1 values. In his case studies, Ross does not adopt an explicitly comparative research strategy that would have involved picking particular cases with a goal of comparing them to other selected cases. Comparative designs allow a researcher to directly ask questions about how aspects that are different (or similar) between cases are associated with different (or similar) causal mechanisms. As we have argued in this book, comparisons are crucial for building knowledge about the substantive X1/Y relationship. In this particular example, one might use the large-N results from Collier and Hoeffler to extend Ross' research by picking additional cases that are strong comparisons to the ones already studied. For example, as a comparison to Indonesia in 1975, one might choose to study Nigeria in 1975, which features a similar X1 value and similar expected relationship, yet Nigeria did not experience a civil conflict. In a comparison such as this one, a researcher might examine whether there are inhibitory mechanisms in the Nigeria case, or study if the mechanism requires some other factor to lead to war that is missing in Nigeria but present in Indonesia. One could use the large-N results to select cases for other comparisons depending on the specific question under study.

7.6 Conclusion

A central theme of this book is that researchers must think creatively about how to use mixed methods to enrich the search for causal mechanisms, as it exists in the often messy world of social science research. Consistent with this broader theme, this chapter recognizes that researchers choose cases for a variety of reasons, not all of which are theoretical, methodological, or even substantive. If a researcher has expertise in a region, speaks the language, has extensive contacts, and access to rich data sources, it is possible to leverage these practical advantages, even if cases are not "optimal" from a purely theoretical or methodological perspective. In these situations, the question is not *whether* to study these cases but instead *how* these cases fit within the broader population of interest and which cases are good candidates for future comparison.

This chapter has explored how researchers can gain perspective on cases they have already selected by using large-N methods and by using the tools discussed in this chapter. These techniques can be used both to help interpret the findings from prior research and to help guide the selection of additional cases to use in comparative designs with prior research. These additional studies might involve full-blown case studies or, if that is not feasible, supplementary analysis based on existing sources. Either way, these additional comparisons can enrich the original case studies. In the case of the analysis by Ross, we believe that Collier and Hoeffler's large-N data enrich his findings (and the search for knowledge about mechanisms) in two ways. First, Ross finds that the mechanisms set forth in the literature are not present in a number of his cases. Our analysis of the large-N data offers some perspective on those findings, suggesting that this was not necessarily because the prior literature is wrong, but because these cases do not feature high levels of the expected X1/Y relationship. Second, consideration of the large-N data might encourage future comparisons centered on interesting puzzles from the perspective of the search for mechanisms, such as why some countries have similar natural resource wealth and expected relationships but different outcomes.

The next chapter discusses this last overarching theme of pathway analysis and possible future studies of mechanisms, and examines how substantive results of pathway analysis can help inform ongoing search for causal mechanisms.

Pathway analysis and future studies of mechanisms

8.1 Introduction

To this point, we have mainly focused on the early stages of mechanism-centered research, particularly selecting cases for pathway analysis that explore the links underlying an association between some explanatory variable (X1) and an outcome (Y). However, the results of pathway analysis not only can provide a map of mechanisms underlying an X1/Y relationship, but also can be used to "look forward" to provide insight into the feasibility and nature of future studies of mechanisms. From this vantage, pathway analysis is best understood as part of a larger research agenda that spans multiple years, multiple research approaches, and multiple researchers.

The forward-looking purposes of pathway analysis are largely ignored in the literature for a variety of possible reasons. Partly this omission may reflect the limited state of knowledge about mechanisms in many areas. Quantitative studies of mechanisms require that a researcher has already identified some basic information about the mechanisms linking X1 and Y and understand the basic structure of the X1/Y relationship (see Table 2.2 in Chapter 2). This omission also may reflect that the literature on how to study mechanisms quantitatively is relatively new and rapidly evolving. Nevertheless, there are some areas in which researchers have accumulated a considerable amount of insight into mechanisms, and there are compelling reasons for pursuing further mechanism-centered research. For researchers working in such an area, the question to ask is: How might insights from pathway analysis inform future studies on mechanisms?

This chapter considers this question in light of the literature on social position or socio-economic standing (SES) and health (disease, mortality rates, longevity, and the like). The literature on SES ($X1$) and health (Y) is an interesting place to explore the forward-looking aspects of pathway analysis for at least two reasons. First, the literature mapping the links between $X1$ and Y is relatively mature, so there are well-developed ideas about the structure of the $X1/Y$ relationship, even if some details of the map remain contested. Second, there are strong policy reasons for studying how specific mechanisms work because direct, significant manipulation of SES through the massive redistribution of wealth seems politically unlikely in the United States. As a result, in the area of SES and health, mechanism-centered research continues with an eye toward developing politically viable, effective policy interventions.

The discussion begins by briefly reviewing the SES and health literature in light of the scenarios set forth in Chapter 2. It then moves to the implications of this literature for three types of post-pathway analysis studies of mechanisms: (1) quantitative studies that seek to use insights about mechanisms to improve confidence that an $X1/Y$ relationship is causal; (2) quantitative studies that seek to estimate the average marginal effect of mechanisms; and (3) what we call "policy-oriented case studies" that examine the conditions under which specific policy interventions are likely to work. The gist is that the complexity of the relationship between SES and health casts serious doubt on the feasibility of meeting the stringent parameters of large-N studies of mechanisms. This does not mean that work on mechanisms should stop. We can envision useful strategies for refocusing the question to engage in further pathway analyses along the lines described in Chapter 5, where we focus on specific sub-links in a longer causal chain related to policy diffusion, or engage in policy-oriented case studies. Even if we find that some types of research are not likely to be implemented, assessing the feasibility of large-N mechanism-centered work represents an important, although underappreciated, contribution to the search for mechanisms, and one that flows naturally from our approach to pathway analysis.

8.2 The literature on SES and health

The literature on SES and health is already vast (and still growing), so this chapter cannot hope to explore all of the literature's nooks and crannies. Instead, it is useful to provide a thumbnail sketch of the part of this scholarship related to two puzzles in the field that have yielded critical insights into the basic structure of the SES–health relationship (Freese and Lutfey 2011; Lutfey and Freese 2005). The first set of studies focuses on health disparities across different populations. Put simply, this literature has repeatedly found that people of lower status live shorter and unhealthier lives (e.g., Chapin 1924; Coombs 1941; Deaton 2002; Marmot 2004; Pappas et al. 1993). Although there are many twists and turns along the way, this finding holds across nearly every age group; across nations; and across a wide range of outcomes, including infant mortality, longevity, developmental problems, disability, and specific diseases (Mechanic 2000, 2002).

Even today, studies show that the negative relationship between some aspects of SES and health in the United States is getting worse. For example, one study finds that life expectancy for college graduates increased 1.6 years from 1990 to 2000, while the life expectancy of those without a college degree during the same period remained flat (Meara et al. 2008). Interestingly, there is a health "gradient" – as opposed to some threshold effect – across populations, so that health inequalities persist well into the middle and upper classes. For example, in a famous set of studies known as the Whitehall Studies, researchers tracked the health of British civil servants over time and found health gaps across civil service ranks, even though all of these officials worked in similar office environments, all enjoyed steady employment, and all were from relatively homogeneous backgrounds (Marmot et al. 1984; Marmot and Shipley 1996).

To explain this puzzle, some researchers have treated SES as a "placeholder" variable and sought to disaggregate it into component parts to trace the pathways connecting various aspects of SES to health outcomes (Link and Phelan 1995). (This exercise is analogous to what we did in Chapter 5 in the policy diffusion example, where we considered how to explore a specific link in a broader causal chain.) This work has yielded a number of critical insights into how SES affects health outcomes. First, the literature identifies a large number of potential mechanisms linking SES and health. Second, researchers have found both positive and negative effects of increased SES. For example, a subject gaining employment should increase his or her SES, and should therefore also increase access to healthcare through the individual's employer (given that this benefit is offered). While this should improve the new employee's health, particular jobs might also increase stress, which is likely to produce negative health outcomes. Third, the health gradient suggests that mechanisms are likely to be heterogeneous and/or function differently across values and effect sizes of SES, so that the mechanisms that create the gap in health outcomes at the lower end of SES are probably different than the ones creating a similar gap at higher levels. It seems likely, for instance, that access to basic health services would be relevant to explaining health disparities between the very poor and wealthy, but other factors would most likely be relevant for understanding any gap between middle and upper-middle classes, both of which presumably have similar access to basic health services.

The literature usefully aggregates these insights into various diagrams that map the links between SES and health, such as the one reproduced in Figure 8.1, which is based on the MacArthur Research Network on SES & Health (Adler and Stewart 2010). This particular figure represents a simplified model of SES and health because the authors, Nancy Adler and Judith Stewart, intentionally omitted feedback loops and

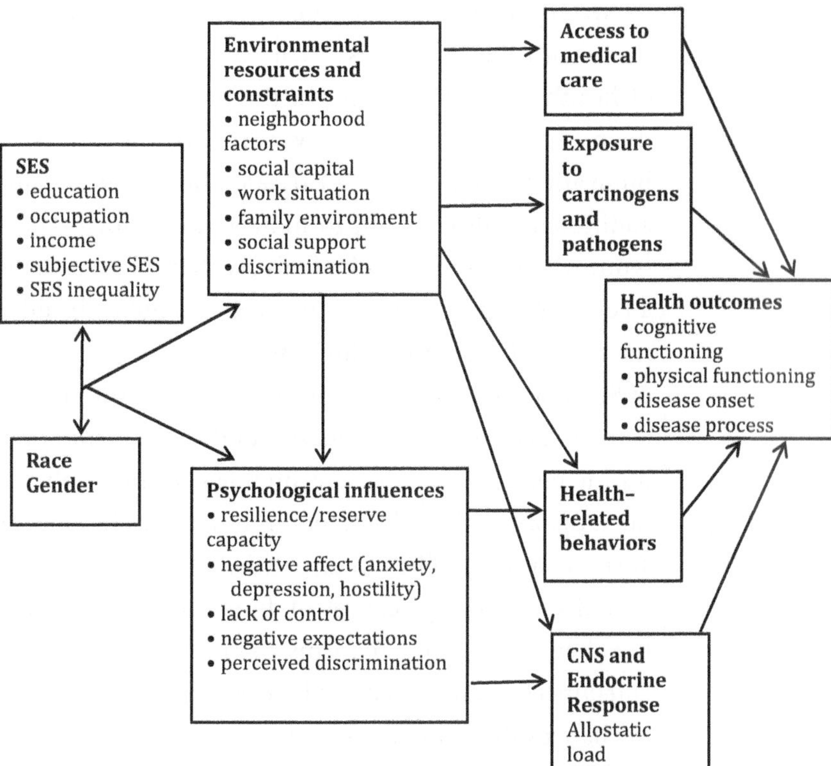

Figure 8.1   Pathways linking SES and health (excluding feedback loops and interaction effects)
Source: From Adler and Stewart (2010).

interaction effects (2010: 11), but still it captures some of the basics of the relationship, which is highly complex.

The second cluster of studies focuses on the persistence of health disparities over time. This has occurred even as health risks have dramatically shifted for large segments of the population, as a result of improvements in the diagnosis and treatment of illnesses, eradication of some diseases, and improvement in public health conditions such as sanitation. This puzzle has led researchers to explore how health disparities across levels of SES recreate themselves over time. One widely cited explanation in the field of medical sociology is the idea of "fundamental cause" (Link and Phelan 1995, 1996, 2002, 2005). The crux of the argument, as articulated by Bruce Link and Jo Phelan, is that those with higher SES use their superior resources to take advantage of health innovations (and in the process maintain the gap between themselves and those with lower SES). By the time the benefits of these innovations have (partially) trickled down, the wealthy are garnering additional health benefits from new innovations. The resulting picture is one where high SES individuals use their *resource advantages* to pursue an ever-changing frontier of medical and public health advances, which maintains the gap in health outcomes, even though people at all levels of SES may be better off in absolute terms. From the perspective of fundamental causation, the "puzzle" of the persistence of health disparities during periods of medical, technological, and public health advances is not a puzzle at all. Indeed, this argument implies that advances in these areas are a *cause* of health disparities.

A distinguishing feature of fundamental causation – as opposed to other, more familiar forms of causation – is the identification of "metamechanisms" that explain why the X1/Y relationship is robust to changes that should affect it (Freese and Lutfey 2011). With respect to SES and health, Jeremy Freese and Karen Lutfey posit four possible metamechanisms that interact with the types of variables set forth in Figure 8.1. The first is their notion of the just-explained resource advantages. But not all metamechanisms, Freese and Lutfey argue, directly relate to the strategic use of greater resources by wealthy individuals.

A second possible metamechanism – *spillovers* – involves where people live. Individuals are embedded in communities, so even if they do not use their own resources to take advantage of the latest health advances, positive attributes in their community may improve their health. For example, a wealthy person might choose to live in a neighborhood for reasons that have nothing to do with health, but it typically happens that more affluent neighborhoods have less exposure to toxins and better access to good healthcare. A third possible metamechanism is *habitus* – basic dispositions of interpretation and action – that implies that some elite practices may engender better health. Freese and Lutfey explain that some researchers have found an emerging cultural imperative to "live one's life like a project" with respect to health. Like many new cultural practices, this is likely to begin as an elite practice that partially filters down to lower classes. The fourth possibility is *institutions*, which may serve as a dynamic link between SES and health. In fact, there are studies that show that the healthcare system works better for those with higher SES. The implication is that all of the variables and mechanisms listed in Figure 8.1 are potentially connected in complex and dynamic ways through the various metamechanisms.

In sum, unlike the previous examples in this book where little is known about mechanisms and the central task is to probe the basic structure of the X1/Y relationship, here there is a relatively good idea about the structure of the SES–health relationship, even if the picture continues to evolve. Returning to the language of Chapter 2, it seems clear that the relationship between SES and health represents a complex variant of scenario 4: a case where the X1/Y relationship features direct and indirect effects and multiple, interactive mechanisms. There are the added wrinkles of positive and negative mechanisms, the likelihood that mechanisms will differ across values and effect sizes of SES, and the idea of metamechanisms that preserve the relationship over time.

8.3   Some key types of future mechanism-centered research

A detailed map of the links between X1 and Y is a significant milestone in the search for mechanisms, but it is not necessarily the final destination. There are at least three types of mechanism-centered research that might grow out of pathway analysis that maps mechanisms: (1) quantitative studies that seek to use insights about mechanisms to improve confidence in the causal nature of an X1/Y relationship; (2) quantitative studies that seek to estimate the average marginal effect of specific mechanisms; and (3) qualitative policy-oriented case studies. Each is discussed in turn.

8.4   Quantitative studies that improve confidence in causality

One potential type of work that can leverage the results from pathway analysis is the study of mechanisms to bolster confidence in the causal nature of a statistical relationship. Researchers interested in this type of work need to eventually satisfy what Judea Pearl (2009) calls the "front-door criterion," which requires one to establish that the X1/Y relationship is analogous to scenario 1 in Chapter 2, the Single Pathway Scenario. Specifically, the front-door criterion requires the following three conditions to be met (Pearl 2009: 83; see also Glynn and Ichino 2012 for an application of the method):

1. The mechanism must capture the entire effect of X1 on Y. This implies that there cannot be a direct effect of X1 on Y that occurs in the absence of the mechanism. The mechanism can have a positive or negative effect, but if there are multiple mechanisms then *all* of them must be either positive or negative. If the mechanisms do not *all* affect the outcome in the same direction, then a researcher has to understand the net effect of each possible combination of mechanisms, which means that observing a single mechanism will be insufficient to make inferences.

2. No other unmeasured variable that can affect the outcome directly affects the mechanism. In other words, there cannot be an unmeasured variable (X2) that both affects the outcome and the mechanism, because if that is the case, then it is possible that X2 is actually the cause of both the mechanism and the outcome, and that they would be observed even in the absence of X1. In this event, the presence of the mechanism would not be informative about the effect of X1 on Y.

3. No other unmeasured variable that affects the mechanism can affect the X1 variable. This means there cannot be a situation in which some other variable can cause both the mechanism and the X1 variable. If

that were the case, then it would suggest that X1 may not actually be the cause of the mechanism, and observing the mechanism and the outcome would not tell if X1 was the cause of both.

The bottom line is that if a researcher wants to improve causal inference about the X1/Y relationship by studying mechanisms, then these three conditions must be met.[1] To do so requires a particular relationship between X1, M, and Y, and it requires that a researcher know that these conditions are met. In the absence of such knowledge, an appropriate goal for pathway analysis is to help understand whether it is possible to achieve these criteria, for example by exploring whether X1 has a direct effect on Y; or if there are multiple mechanisms between X1 and Y, and, if so, whether they are all positive or negative.

If researchers can identify when the direct effect is absent and if the mechanisms are universally positive or negative, then scholars may be able to treat the identification of any mechanism between X1 and Y as "as if sufficient" to improve confidence in the underlying X1/Y relationship, because even if we cannot observe all the mechanisms, we can safely assume that observing a single mechanism is associated with a positive or negative effect (see Glynn and Ichino 2012).[2] Unless both of these conditions can be met, achieving the front-door criterion is not possible. Although disappointing, this conclusion is useful as it can guide future research by ruling out particular avenues of inquiry.

Returning to SES, it is useful to consider the *simplified* model in Figure 8.1. Based on this model, nine different possible variables (listed in bold) related to various health outcomes have been identified

---

[1] The front-door criterion does not require the presence of the mechanism in all cases where the key explanatory variable occurs; that is, there may still be an average effect of the X1 variable on the outcome even if not *every* treated unit features the mechanism.

[2] In this case the mechanism can be some type of aggregate mechanism as long as all the mechanisms are positive or negative, because in that situation inferences about X/Y relationship do not change whether one or all of the mechanisms are observed.

(assuming race and gender are treated as separate variables). The primary key explanatory variable is the overarching concept of SES, and the other highlighted variables can be considered mechanisms that affect the pathway between SES and health. Remember also that not all of these links act either positively or negatively as SES increases. While most of these links improve health as SES increases, some may have negative effects. In addition, Figure 8.1 sets aside issues of feedback loops and interaction among the various variables and mechanisms.

Even if we accept this map of the SES–health relationship, which Adler and Stewart themselves concede is a simplification, we cannot meet the front-door criterion. There are multiple mechanisms and they are not all positive or negative. If these mechanisms interact, as the authors suggest, these interactions provide another barrier to meeting the front-door criterion. The bottom line is that the front-door criterion simply cannot be satisfied in the area of SES and health, unless we believed that there were specific values of SES or effect sizes where there was only one mechanism or only positive or negative mechanisms. This seems unlikely, given what we know about the interactive and dynamic nature of these mechanisms across populations and over time.

8.5 Quantitative studies that seek to estimate the average marginal effect of a mechanism

If scholars are instead interested in identifying the average effect of a mechanism using large-N research, then they need to build a different type of study. A basic framework for identifying the average effect of a mechanism was outlined by psychologists Reuben M. Baron and David A. Kenney (1986), but recently other scholars have identified a set of more general statistical techniques to identify the average effect of mechanisms and have also discussed how research designs can aid in this endeavor (Imai et al. 2013). As Imai and colleagues (2011) explain, estimating the effect of a mechanism requires that we meet the "sequential ignorability assumption."[3] In essence, a researcher must disentangle the mechanisms from one another and from the treatment so that independent effect of the mechanism(s) can be estimated. This requirement is simple enough in the abstract, but it poses a considerable challenge in practice, because it requires that the mechanisms are identified, their relationship to each other and the treatment is understood, and both the treatment and the mechanism(s) are randomized to ensure that the independent effect of each is known (for more on this, see Imai et al. 2011, 2013).

In lieu of actual randomization it may be possible to achieve "as if" randomization of both treatment and mechanism via statistical techniques. This requires a statistical model and appropriate measures for modeling the assignment of both the treatment and the level of the mechanism. Both actual and "as if" randomization are difficult to achieve, but for now we'll focus on how the relationship between X1, M1, and Y complicates the ability to disentangle the relationship between X1 and M1. For example, if particular values of M1 only occur with particular values of X1, then there is no independence of X1 and M1, and how much of X1's effect on Y is direct or indirect via the mechanism cannot be disentangled.[4] In the pursuit of sequential ignorability, pathway analysis can shed light on the number of mechanisms, their relationships to each other, and to situations in which a researcher might be able to disentangle mechanisms from each other either via research design or statistical approaches.[5] Often it will be impossible to meet the

---

[3] The idea of ignorability in treatment assignment was developed by Don Rubin and Paul Rosenbaum in a series of papers during the 1970s and 1980s (Rosenbaum and Rubin 1983, 1984).

[4] Our treatment of sequential ignorability and its implications is admittedly very brief. Our main goal is only to provide a basic sense of the analytic requisites of estimating the effects of mechanisms and then to consider how pathway analysis might help assessing the feasibility of meeting these parameters.

[5] Imai and Yamamoto (2013) discuss some of the challenges in meeting sequential ignorability in the presence of multiple mechanisms and provide additional guidance about how to statistically identify the average effect of a mechanism when

requirements of sequential ignorability, so researchers will instead want to conduct sensitivity analyses regarding the effects of X1 and M1 (Imai et al. 2011, 2013), and pathway analysis may be useful in helping to calibrate the analyses. The basic idea of a sensitivity analysis is to assess how the estimated effect of a causal mechanism depends on its correlation with either the treatment or another mechanism, and a crucial piece of sensitivity analysis is to identify the relevant amount of correlation that exists. Given that it is often not known how likely it is to observe mechanisms occurring at the same time or how the level of a mechanism depends on the treatment, it may be that pathway analysis, with a handful (or two) of well-chosen cases, can help a researcher to better understand the correlations between treatment and mechanism(s) and therefore help to calibrate sensitivity analyses. In general, the great difficulty with fully disentangling treatment and mechanism(s) from one another means that scholars will often need to rely on sensitivity analyses in making claims about the effect of different mechanisms and pathway analysis may help identify a range of correlations that seem likely to exist in a given situation.

This type of analysis is potentially salient to the field of SES and health, where understanding how specific mechanisms function remains a critical topic in the literature. As David Mechanic argued more than ten years ago:

It has long been established that individuals' location in society predicts their life chances, health, and longevity. This observation now is the focus of a growing and sophisticated literature in the United States and abroad seeking to understand the pathways through which income, wealth, education, occupation, and other features of social rank influence health status and mortality. The observation itself is unassailable, but good social policy requires detailed understanding of the dynamics through which these outcomes occur. (2002: 48)

there are multiple mechanisms and how they may interact. It is noteworthy that these authors confine themselves to experimental situations in which there is greater ability to manipulate the treatment and mechanism than in an observational setting.

However, the prospects for understanding the average effect of a particular mechanism are remote, because it will be nearly impossible to meet the conditions of sequential ignorability. To understand why, consider Figure 8.1 and the different ways that the variables (ignoring the metamechanisms) can interact with one another. To understand the interactions, first a researcher must think about whether the mechanisms are continuous or categorical; and if categorical, how many different categories exist. It is important to think about these issues, because to understand the independent effect of a mechanism, a mechanism must be disentangled from both the treatment and other mechanisms. If a given mechanism cannot be separated from some other mechanism(s), then how that mechanism functions in the absence of the other mechanism(s) is an unknown. Therefore, for the sake of understanding the average effect of a mechanism, a researcher must be able to isolate (either experimentally or statistically) each mechanism. If it is believed that each of the nine main variables (again, treating gender and race as distinct although they appear in the same box in the figure) has two possible levels, then there are a total of 512 possible combinations of these variables. To compute the number of combinations of mechanisms requires identifying the number of mechanisms and the number of levels of each. In this simplified example, there are 2^9 combinations.

Of course, it may be that some of the variables have more than two possible values. For example, even if it is believed that gender takes only two values and it is assumed that the other eight variables can take on only four values – which is debatable, as some are continuous variables – there are 131,072 possible combinations: the eight variables with four levels lead to 65,536 possible combinations, and each combination can occur for both men and women leading to $2*(4^8)$ combinations. Quite quickly it becomes clear that the possible combinations of treatment and mechanisms explode to an unmanageable number. Even if there were sufficient individual cases, which might be possible for studies of SES and health, the difficulty of studying all of these combinations is prohibitive.

To further illustrate the difficulty of studying this many mechanisms, Adler and Stewart (2010) conceived of SES and each of the eight listed aggregated mechanisms as containing a variety of subcategories. If it is determined that these subcategories are appropriate units of study, that leads to 22 different factors to analyze. Even if each of these 22 factors has only two possible levels (high versus low, rich versus poor, access versus no access), this leads to more than four million possible combinations (2^{22}). If each factor has three possible values, then there are a total of more than 31 billion possible combinations (3^{22}). This clearly exceeds anyone's ability to identify the independent effects of mechanisms, because it is highly unlikely a researcher will find enough cases to populate all of the possible cells or have the time, energy, or ability to conduct this many case studies.

An even deeper problem exists if it is presumed that the mechanisms are not actually independent from one another, but occur in various combinations. This may reduce the number of possible combinations of mechanisms, but it also eliminates the possibility of finding the independent effects of any one mechanism. This problem is further compounded by the argument in Lutfey and Freese (2005) about the presence of metamechanisms. These metamechanisms are said to maintain the basic SES and health outcome relationship even if/when mechanisms that underlie the relationship are modified. This has a significant implication for studying mechanisms. The mechanisms in Figure 8.1 may not have independent effects because of these metamechanisms, and therefore the premise of sequential ignorability is flawed in this context.

Our reading of the literature in light of the scenarios from Table 2.2 suggests that in studying the relationship between SES and health, it will be nearly impossible to identify the independent effects of mechanisms. Furthermore, even performing sensitivity analyses will be difficult because of both the number of mechanisms and the relationships among them. As noted earlier, it will also be impossible to meet the front-door criterion if the literature is correct in its identification of multiple positive and negative mechanisms, and interactions among mechanisms and metamechanisms. The implication is that these types of large-N studies of mechanisms are not feasible. This may be disappointing at some level, but it is a significant contribution because eliminating avenues of inquiry is a valuable addition to the store of useful knowledge.

Research finding that there is no possible way to reasonably satisfy the front-door criterion or sequential ignorability does not mean that the study of mechanisms should be abandoned. In the context of SES and health, it is, quite frankly, simply too important an area to ignore. It does mean, however, that researchers must make some choices about why a study of mechanisms in this domain is being undertaken and what it is hoped to be learned in such research, while remembering to be circumspect in interpreting any findings.

One choice is to move away from studying SES and health and toward targeting specific links on the known chain of variables and mechanisms. This would involve deciding where to cut the causal chain based on what are the most interesting and practical considerations, such as data availability. For example, one might decide to focus on the links between access to medical care and disease onset. This would bring the researcher to issues similar to policy diffusion, with the goal of exploring the relationship between sub-links that are more likely to meet the front-door criterion or sequential ignorability.

This choice, however, moves the researcher away from studying SES and health, which might not be acceptable. For those interested in untangling how various metamechanisms work over time and interact with the wide range of factors listed in Figure 8.1, cutting the causal chain into short, disconnected links would be substantively counterproductive. However, if the ultimate goal is to implement a study that meets either the front-door criterion or sequential ignorability, then the only plausible approach is to cut the X1/Y relationship into smaller chains where the relationship may be simpler and, thus, more likely to meet the narrow analytic requisites of large-N mechanism-centered work.

8.6   Policy-oriented case studies

The third approach is to reconsider the goals of the underlying research agenda and to pursue policy-oriented case studies. In the area of SES and health, one likely goal is to focus on what policy-relevant knowledge can be gleaned via the study of mechanisms in specific contexts, which may differ from the knowledge needed for social scientific studies (Cartwright and Hardie 2012). Specifically, even if it is not possible to satisfy sequential ignorability and to estimate the average effect of specific mechanisms, understanding if and how to manipulate the SES and health relationship remains important to many different actors (for example, governments, insurance companies, medical providers, and so on). To manipulate this relationship usually requires intervening in a way that affects one (or more) of the mechanisms linking SES to health. If the goal is to generate policy-relevant information about causal mechanisms, then carefully thinking about which mechanisms to study and under what conditions to study a given mechanism(s) is a vital first step. Based on the given goal, the aim would be to gain three primary types of knowledge. First, a researcher will need to establish whether policy interventions are able to manipulate particular mechanisms. Second, it will be necessary to figure out if a particular policy intervention affects the SES–health relationship. Third, the context in which the intervention took place will need to be understood. This will be useful whether the researcher suspects that the intervention worked or failed.

This type of work is consistent with the prescriptions of Nancy Cartwright and Jeremy Hardie (2012), who argue that all empirical results about the success of policy intervention depend on *ceteris paribus* claims: claims about the conditions under which policies are effective. Even policies supported by studies using the gold standard of a randomized policy intervention still require a *ceteris paribus* claim, because the effect may only occur under particular conditions. Therefore, even if a researcher can identify a policy intervention that worked in a particular context, it is still necessary to understand, as much as possible, whether the intervention that worked in one situation is likely to work in another. This implies a slightly different way to conduct multi-method research. In particular, it might be useful to identify a prior policy intervention that seemed to have the intended effects and then use in-depth case studies to try to understand both what made the intervention successful (which mechanisms did it modify) and to understand the context of the intervention (what is contained in a typical *ceteris paribus* claim).

The ability to understand the conditions in which policy interventions succeed is likely to be greater if a researcher conducts multiple case studies of similar policy interventions, so that any similarities across the different instances of a successful policy intervention can be identified. These similarities may provide some purchase over what might be relevant in assessing when a policy is likely to work. It may also be useful to study similar policy interventions that failed to achieve the desired results, and then use these cases to try to understand the failure. This information can give insight into what conditions must be in place for the intervention to succeed.

Based on the information learned in case studies regarding the conditions associated with a successful intervention, it is possible to design a policy experiment to test whether the same intervention meets the *ceteris paribus* claim. The goal would be to select cases (clinics, geographic areas, and so on) into the sample and then develop a randomization protocol that allows intervention in a random subset of the cases initially selected. If the results continue to suggest that the policy intervention manipulated the mechanism(s) in question and that the intervention changed the SES–health relationship, then there would be increased confidence in understanding the conditions related to when a policy intervention works. This is broadly analogous to what Alexander L. George and Andrew Bennett (2005) discuss in their treatment of using case studies to build hypotheses about the analytic boundaries of existing theory.

Although not framed in these terms, Lutfey and Freese's (2005) ethnographic study of diabetes treatment in two clinics approaches the kind of qualitative work that is consistent with a research agenda aimed at building useful policy insights and later experimental work. The empirical study involved a year-long ethnographic analysis of diabetes care in two endocrinology clinics in the same university-based healthcare system. One (the "Park Clinic") served primarily white middle- and upper-class patients; the other (the "County Clinic") served largely minority working-class patients. The study used a combination of observations, interviews, and surveys to gather data on the differences with respect to four clusters of mechanisms: (1) mechanisms inside the clinics related to their organizational practices and resources (e.g., continuity of care, in-clinic educational resources, and division of labor among doctors); (2) mechanisms external to the clinic (e.g., patients' financial limitations, occupational constraints, and social support networks); (3) mechanisms related to patients' dispositions, including their apparent motivation (e.g., cost of compliance with a treatment regime, relative magnitude of lifestyle adjustments); and (4) apparent cognitive ability (e.g., interactional differences and capacities as practical achievements).

The goal of Lutfey and Freese's ethnographic study was to provide thick descriptions of how the multiple pathways interact and gain some insights into the broader concept of fundamental causation. However, one could easily reinterpret some of their findings as providing the types of *ceteris paribus* insights identified by Cartwright and Hardie. According to Lutfey and Freese, the Park Clinic had much greater continuity of care, which is seen as critical to adherence to treatment regimens. Specifically, the authors found that the continuity of care at the Park Clinic produced a much greater quality of information to doctors in determining and assessing treatments. From a policy perspective, it would be tempting to regulate clinics to ensure greater continuity of care (for example, by requiring that each patient regularly see the same doctor and nurse on their visits, or requiring the maintenance of low provider–patient ratios).

However, the authors warn that this would not necessarily result in improved health outcomes: "While our data are taken from two very different diabetes clinics, our inquiry should not be taken as suggesting that all mechanisms would be eliminated if the patients we observed were treated at the same clinic. To the contrary, we assert that a series of additional phenomena would continue to pattern health outcomes according to SES" (Lutfey and Freese 2005: 1348). One of their examples involves the role of individual patients' financial constraints. Regardless of the degree of continuity of care, it is critical that patients with diabetes test their glucose levels regularly, but the strips for testing are not always covered by insurance programs. Not surprisingly, patients with less disposable income often cut back on their testing, which undermines the quality of information available to the attending healthcare providers, whether or not they see the same doctors.

The policy implication is that for continuity of care to improve health outcomes for all populations, it would be important to account for the financial constraints of patients and to provide testing materials that are not covered by existing programs. This insight falls far short of what is needed to model the interactions among these variables, but it would surely be useful for policymakers as they assess how to improve diabetes care among the poor; one possible solution might be to combine a regulation that requires the adoption of organizational practices from the "best" clinics, with additional support for uncovered costs related to patient treatments. If it appears that combining continuity of care with the provision of free testing materials has an effect at the County Clinic, then this policy response could be ramped up as policymakers and healthcare professionals build toward a policy study featuring randomized interventions.

8.7   Conclusion

The focus of this book is to provide guidance in using pathway analysis to better understand some association between an explanatory variable

(X1) and an outcome (Y) by mapping unobserved links between them and by identifying the basic structure of the relationship in light of the scenarios discussed in Chapter 2. We suspect that this type of analysis will dominate given the limited understanding of mechanisms in many fields. This chapter, however, illustrates some of the "forward-looking" purposes of pathway analysis; in other words, the ways in which pathway analysis might inform future studies of mechanisms once the basic structure of an X1/Y relationship has been mapped.

Using the literature on SES and health, which is relatively mature, we have considered how pathway analysis can relate to future studies of mechanisms. Several lessons from this chapter are worth highlighting. First, quantitative studies of mechanisms require that a researcher meet precise assumptions before attempting to apply these techniques. If using mechanisms to improve confidence in the causal nature of an X1/Y relationship, it is important to satisfy the front-door criterion. If estimating the average marginal effect of specific mechanisms, then satisfying sequential ignorability is also important. Both are stringent parameters, so they may be hard to meet given the complex relationships studied by social scientists.

Second, the feasibility of meeting the front-door criterion or sequential ignorability flows naturally from mapping X1/Y relationships using the scenarios in Chapter 2 (see Table 8.1 for a summary of common scenarios, front-door criterion, and sequential ignorability). Moreover, meeting these parameters will likely be quite difficult in a world of multiple causal pathways between variables and outcomes. This is not because of any inherent limitation of case studies or pathway analysis, but because the front-door criterion is hard to meet outside of scenario 1, the Single Pathway Scenario, in which there is a single path and a single mechanism. This means that researchers should be very careful if claiming that combining large-N regression analysis with some process-tracing case studies helps "establish" causality. It does not. It can, however, help one to understand the nature of the relationship among the variables, mechanisms, and outcomes, which, in turn, can help assess

Table 8.1 Summary of the relationships between the common scenarios and the front-door criterion and sequential ignorability

Scenario (brief description)	Is meeting the front-door criterion possible?	Is meeting sequential ignorability possible?
Scenario 1 (Single Pathway)	Yes	No
Scenario 2 (Direct and Indirect Pathways)	No, unless we can identify where there are no direct effects of X1 on Y	Yes
Scenario 3 (Multiple Exclusive Pathways)	No, unless we can identify where there are no direct effects of X1 on Y *and* all mechanisms are either positive or negative	Yes, provided that the number of combinations to be studied is not prohibitive
Scenario 4 (Multiple Non-Exclusive Pathways)	No, unless we can identify where there are no direct effects of X1 on Y *and* all mechanisms and their interactions are either positive or negative	Yes, provided that the number of combinations to be studied is not prohibitive

whether it is possible to meet the front-door criterion. Similarly, the scenarios imply that building toward sequential ignorability will also be challenging, because it requires a deep understanding of how the variables, mechanisms, and outcome interact and, as seen with SES and health, it is possible to quickly become overwhelmed when the numbers of variables and mechanisms (and their measures) grow.

Finally, as stressed in the last chapter, researchers should not make the perfect the enemy of the good. Just because it is not possible to fully map out the various mechanisms that link an X1 to Y, or to satisfy the front-door criterion or sequential ignorability, does not mean the use of case studies to explore mechanisms should be abandoned, particularly in a situation such as SES and health in which policy stakes for identifying mechanisms are so high. Policymakers will continue to seek solutions even if the knowledge does not reach the highest standards of causal inference, and therefore researchers should help them to understand what policies are likely to work and under what conditions. Faced with the reality of the complexities of studying a relationship like SES and health, a researcher should either seek to focus on specific links in the known causal chain, and thus help generate knowledge about sub-links that have not been explored, or seek to focus on case studies of the relationship in specific settings with an eye toward generating useful policy-oriented information about the relationship in particular contexts and the likely conditions under which certain actions seem promising. This knowledge will not approach what is needed to satisfy the analytic requisites of the latest estimation techniques, but it can provide insights that can be incorporated into later, randomized experiments.

9 Conclusion

9.1 Putting the pieces together

This book has examined pathway analysis from a number of angles: how to prepare for it by reading the literature in light of its analytic requisites and different ideal types of X1/Y relationships; how to select cases for it based on the expected X1/Y relationships and variation in case characteristics; how to use these tools to gain perspective on cases already selected for process tracing; and how the results from pathway analysis might inform future studies of mechanisms. This chapter seeks to put these pieces together and review the role of pathway analysis in a continuing mixed-method research agenda on mechanisms. The argument is that pathway analysis serves as a critical bridge from what we know about an X1/Y relationship through large-N studies to detailed maps of the mechanisms connecting X1 and Y, which can be used to assess the feasibility of future quantitative studies of mechanisms and the appropriate goals of future qualitative work on mechanisms. From this perspective, good pathway analysis advances the search for mechanisms by systematically building on what we already know about the X1/Y relationship, generating insights into the links between variables, and clarifying avenues of future inquiry.

9.2 The role of pathway analysis in the mixed-methods search for mechanisms

A central theme of the book is that pathway analysis constitutes a distinct mode of inquiry. Whereas most research in the social sciences seeks to understand the causes of events or estimate average effects of some variable, X1, on an outcome, Y (Mahoney and Goertz 2006), pathway analysis seeks to (1) understand the mechanisms underlying the X1/Y relationship in particular cases and (2) generate insights from these cases about mechanisms in the unstudied population of cases featuring the X1/Y relationship. By its very nature, pathway analysis connects the literature on the X1/Y relationship to an ongoing, mixed-method research agenda that first seeks to map mechanisms so that we have a better understanding of the X1/Y relationship and then seeks to inform future, mechanism-centered work.

Figure 9.1 lays out a schematic overview of the role of pathway analysis in this type of research agenda. As noted in Chapter 2, the research agenda begins with large-N studies that establish a robust relationship between X1 and Y, controlling for other factors (represented in the first box in Figure 9.1). This association between variables, however, is not enough to fully understand the X1/Y relationship for methodological, substantive, or policy reasons. We need to ascertain *how* X1 generates Y.

Exploring the unobserved links between X1 and Y is the primary task of pathway analysis. In preparing for pathway analysis – moving from the first box in Figure 9.1 to the second – scholars must determine whether the literature does, in fact, establish a robust association between X1 and Y controlling for other factors (X2) and provides the necessary data to implement our case selection method. At a minimum, these data would include measures of the X1, X2, and Y values in particular cases and allow us, where applicable, to estimate the expected relationship in specific cases using the appropriate method. Assuming these basic analytic requisites are met, scholars need to review the literature in light of the scenarios set forth in Chapter 2 to determine what is known (and not known) about the X1/Y relationship (and the relevant measurement issues) and, by extension, what types of questions should be asked in the field. These scenarios are intended as heuristic devices – touchstones not rigid categories – for organizing and aggregating insights about the X1/Y relationship that are likely to be implicit and spread across many studies.

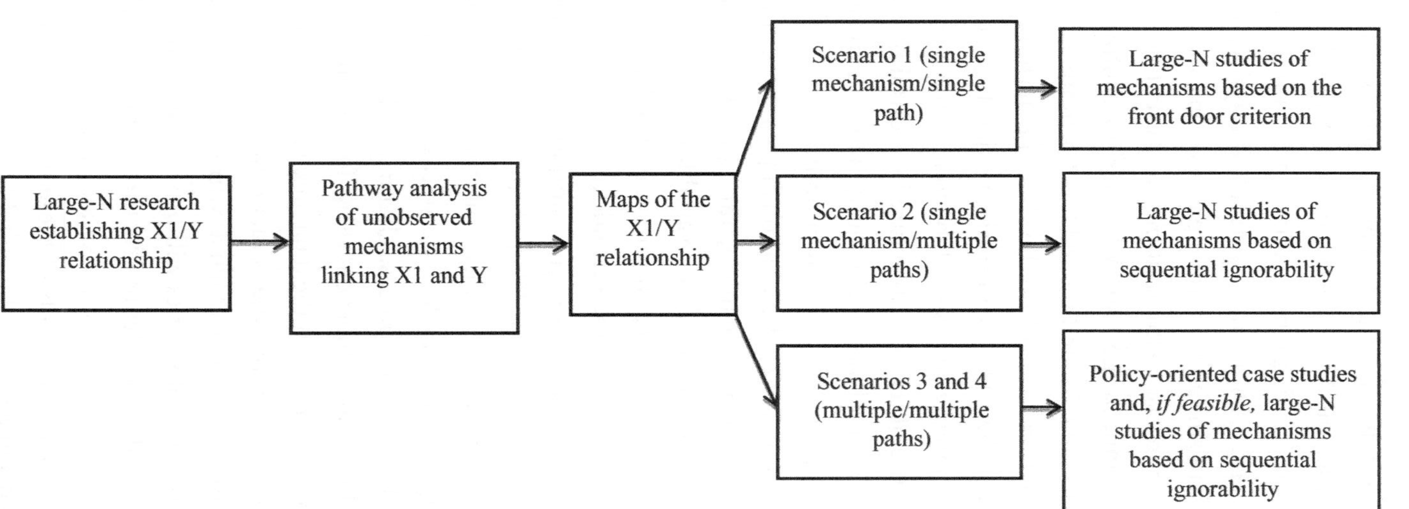

Figure 9.1   The role of pathway analysis in mechanism-centered research agendas

They include the following: cases where there is a single mechanism and single path connecting X1 and Y (scenario 1, Single Pathway Scenario); cases where there is a single mechanism but multiple paths connecting X1 and Y (scenario 2, Direct and Indirect Pathways); cases with multiple, exclusive mechanisms and multiple paths (scenario 3, Multiple Exclusive Pathways); and cases with multiple, non-exclusive mechanisms and multiple paths connecting X1 and Y (scenario 4, Multiple Non-Exclusive Pathways). (See Table 2.2 and related text for more detail.)

In many instances, we will not be able to determine which scenario best encapsulates the X1/Y relationship. Under these circumstances, the central goal of pathway analysis will be to map the X1/Y relationship to gain a better sense of its basic structure by ascertaining which scenario applies. Critical areas of inquiry, in addition to issues related to measurement, will be (1) the number (or lower bound estimates) of mechanisms connecting X1 and Y; (2) the relationships among mechanisms; and (3) the extent to which mechanisms (and how they function) relate to the values of other key explanatory variables and possible confounds.

Pathway analysis, of course, cannot generate reliable maps of the X1/Y relationships – move from the second to the third box in Figure 9.1 – unless we select promising cases in a transparent manner that facilitates the aggregation of knowledge. There is no simple algorithm for doing this. Instead, we must build on existing theory and empirics, adopt a comparative approach, and select sets of cases that feature the expected X1/Y relationship and vary on case characteristics. Using these criteria, scholars should visualize their data (by, for instance, creating scatterplots) and look for puzzles in the data (such as cases where the expected relationship is the same but the actual outcomes differ) and opportunities to exercise case control (such as within-case variation over time). Analyzing these types of puzzles will provide opportunities to generate hypotheses about the underlying structure of the X1/Y relationship and, eventually, map the links between X1 and Y.

While filling in all the details of these maps might never be done in some areas and some links will inevitably remain contested, we should be able to assess the basic structure of the X1/Y relationship as studies on pathways accumulate. In the case of SES and health, for instance, the search for mechanisms continues and the nature of fundamental causation remains disputed, but it seems reasonably clear that the pathways between SES and health are highly complex and interactive and thus represent an intricate version of scenario 4 – Multiple Non-Exclusive Pathways. Knowing the basic structure of the X1/Y relationship even without all the details in place can be very useful to scholars interested in pursuing further mechanism-centered research (moving beyond the third box in Figure 9.1). For instance, if scenario 1 (Single Pathway Scenario) applies, we can design studies that satisfy the front-door criterion and hence improve our confidence in the causal nature of the X1/Y relationship. If scenario 2 (Direct and Indirect Pathways Scenario) applies, we cannot meet the front-door criterion because the mechanism does not capture the entire effect between X1 and Y. We can, however, design studies that satisfy sequential ignorability and estimate the average effect of particular mechanism, as long as we have the relevant measures and data. As the number of mechanisms and their interactions increase and scenarios 3 or 4 apply, we can quickly become overwhelmed and meeting this assumption becomes very unlikely as discussed in Chapter 8 with the SES and health example.

Finding that the front-door criterion or sequential ignorability cannot be satisfied may be frustrating at some level, because it precludes the use of some promising quantitative research techniques. However, knowing that approaches cannot be used is useful in the search for mechanisms, as it allows us to rule out some future avenues of inquiry and focus on others. Specifically, if the structure of the X1/Y relationship is too complex to meet the front-door criterion or sequential ignorability, we need not end our research on mechanisms. We can, instead, turn our attention to studying specific sub-links in the causal chain and/or conducting the policy-oriented case studies. So, in the area of SES and health, the need to fashion policy interventions based on detailed knowledge of the X1/Y relationship is simply too strong to abandon research on mechanisms.

Given this imperative, we should pursue case studies that generate the type of context-specific knowledge that would be useful to policymakers as they try to develop ways to intervene in the complex landscape of health disparities, especially knowledge about the conditions under which particular actions affect mechanisms and when shifts in mechanisms seems to affect the outcome. This knowledge is central to making *ceteris paribus* claims, which are critical to designing effective policies.

9.3   What is good pathway analysis?

Understanding how pathway analysis fits within a broader research agenda on mechanisms helps place its contributions in perspective, which, in turn, helps us assess what constitutes good pathway analysis. First, good pathway analysis builds on the existing theory, empirical knowledge, *and* the large-N scholarship systematically by assessing the gaps in our understanding of the structure of the $X1/Y$ relationship so that we know what types of knowledge we hope to glean from our fieldwork. Second, good pathway analysis is comparative and selects cases based on the expected relationship in the existing literature and variation in case characteristics. The goal is to select cases that present interesting puzzles, such as why cases with similar expected relationships feature different observed results. Is it because there is a mechanism in one case that blocks the relationship or is the expected relationship incorrect in some way? Third, the resulting map of mechanisms between $X1$ and Y from good pathway analysis should be useful to scholars interested in future studies of mechanisms, so that these maps can be used to assess the feasibility of meeting the front-door criterion and/or sequential ignorability and determine whether we need to adjust the goals of further qualitative work. In short, good pathway analysis meaningfully advances the research cycle by increasing our substantive understanding of the unobserved links underlying an $X1/Y$ relationship *and* shedding light on the feasibility and purposes of future mechanism-centered studies.

The negative implication is that good pathway analysis does not yield – nor should it be expected to yield – the types of findings that we would expect from studies at the far end of Figure 9.1. Good pathway analysis produces maps of the X1/Y relationship as case studies accumulate; it does not improve our confidence in the causal nature of X1/Y relationship in the same way that a study that meets the front-door criterion could. Similarly, good pathway analysis does not allow us to estimate the average marginal effects of any single mechanism as a study that meets sequential ignorability could. (It might add insights into how and when a mechanism can be effectively manipulated in particular settings, but that is a very different type of knowledge than its average marginal effects.) We should not allow the pull of the audience in the social sciences, which often places a high premium on establishing causal relationships and estimating average effects, to obscure the essential contributions of pathway analysis nor should we allow this pull to encourage us to overstate what we can learn from it.

9.4 The continuing search for causal mechanisms

Whatever one thinks of our approach to pathway analysis, the search for causal mechanisms in the social sciences will continue because the question of how explanatory variables generate outcomes is crucially important. This partly reflects methodological concerns. We know that correlation is not enough to establish causation and that standard regression analyses applied to observational data are a useful but limited tool in our quest for fully explaining complex causal phenomenon. If we want to offer a convincing account of policy diffusion, for instance, it is not enough to know that when some countries adopt liberal economic policies others do the same at a later time; we need to explain how policies diffuse across national borders. Indeed, it is now *de rigueur* to include some account of how one variable generates another in making causal explanations. In the words of David Waldner (2007: 146), "Explanatory propositions are distinguished from non-explanatory propositions by the inclusion of causal mechanisms" (see also Mayntz 2004: 14; Kiser and Hechter 1991: 5).

Mechanisms also matter for substantive and policy reasons. If we want to assess critical questions about the rule of law in Supreme Court decision-making, it is not enough to know that there is a robust relationship between justices' political ideologies and their votes. We need to understand how ideology versus laws shapes judicial decision-making. If we want to develop effective policy interventions to ameliorate the "oil curse" or health disparities, it is not enough to know that there is an association between natural resource abundance and civil conflict or low SES and poor health outcomes, because we are not in a position to quickly change a country's natural resource wealth or radically redistribute wealth for health purposes (which may be ineffective anyway if we accept the fundamental causation argument about how metamechanisms maintain health disparities over time). We need to know how these things are related, look for mechanisms that can be effectively manipulated through politically viable policies, identify when mechanisms can be manipulated, and understand how mechanisms affect the relevant outcomes.

Moreover, given the growth of large datasets and computing power, we expect more and more findings of associations between variables and outcomes. These empirical regularities will inevitably raise the question of how one explanatory variable generates an outcome controlling for other factors. We also expect that, although there are many ways to study causal mechanisms, scholars interested in mechanisms will often turn to mixed methods in an attempt to leverage the recognized strengths and weaknesses of standard quantitative and qualitative work. It seems undeniable that large-N analysis is well suited for identifying broad patterns in the data while small-N studies are apt for tracing processes that connect variables in specific cases and generating hypotheses about mechanisms in the broader population of cases that feature the relationship of interest. Mixed-method approaches are also appealing because they build on familiar tools, so that we do not need to learn new methods in our search for mechanisms but rather we need to figure out how to combine existing methods creatively and effectively. We hope that this book has contributed to our understanding of how to do this and will encourage more work on using mixed-method research to search for causal mechanisms.

Glossary of terms

Case. Single units observed at a specific time or over a specific period of time with the goal of offering insight into a population of cases.

Case control strategies. A purposive/intentional case selection technique in which researchers choose cases that differ in the outcome, but are otherwise as similar as possible except for a proposed causal variable. Essentially, a case control approach begins with the researcher knowing that the two cases (or groups of cases) differ in their outcome and the researcher attempts to understand why. Ideally, the cases are similar in relevant characteristics other than the key explanatory variable that is under investigation.

Case selection. The process by which units are chosen for analysis. See also case and case study.

Case study. Intensive analyses of single units observed at a specific time or over a specific period of time with the goal of offering insight into a population of cases.

Causal distance. Refers to the proximity of an explanatory variable, X_1, to an outcome Y in a causal chain. By definition, the mechanisms connecting X_1 and Y are "causally closer" to Y than X_1.

Causal effect. The impact that an explanatory variable, X_1, has on an outcome, Y, as in a change in X_1 caused a change in Y.

Causal inference. The analytic process of reaching insights about causation based on observations.

Causal mechanism. See mechanism.

Causal pathways. The process that links X_1 to Y in a given case or across cases. The pathway consists of causal mechanism(s) and intervening variables. See Figure 1.1. See also mechanism.

Causal-process observations. Data that contribute to our understanding of an unobserved process or mechanism linking X_1 and Y.

Comparative pathway analysis.   A method of selecting multiple cases for pathway analysis in light of the expected relationship criteria and variation in case characteristics. See also expected relationship criteria, variation in case characteristics, and pathway analysis.

Control variable.   Variable that is not the focus of the comparative pathway analysis, but that is used to make observations comparable.

Dependent variable.   An outcome to be explained.

Equifinality.   In general, equifinality means multiple causes of an outcome. In the context of pathway analysis, it is the presence of multiple mechanisms between the explanatory variable (X1) and outcome of interest (Y).

Expected relationship criterion.   One of two factors in determining case selection for pathway analysis, which means the degree to which individual cases are expected to feature the relationship of interest between X1 and Y, given existing theory, empirical knowledge, and large-N studies. See also variation in case characteristic criterion.

Explanatory variable.   A factor that has a causal effect on an outcome (or, that helps to explain/predict an outcome).

External validity.   The degree to which a causal inference or hypothesis for a specific set of cases or sample is correct for the unstudied population of cases from which the sample is drawn.

Front-door criterion.   An analytic requirement for large-N studies that seek to use knowledge about mechanisms to probe the causal nature of an X1/Y relationship. Specifically it requires three conditions to be met: (1) the mechanism must capture the entire effect of X1 on Y; (2) no other unmeasured variable that can affect the outcome directly affects the mechanism; and (3) no other unmeasured variable that affects the mechanism can affect the X1 variable.

Hypothesis.   In the context of pathway analysis, it is a falsifiable proposition about the links or mechanisms connecting X1 and Y.

Internal validity.   The degree to which a causal inference about the effect of X1 on Y in a specific set of cases or sample is correct for that sample. Contrast with external validity.

Intervening variable.   An explanatory variable that occurs closer to the dependent variable and is itself caused by another explanatory variable.

An intervening variable may or may not be considered a mechanism. *See also* explanatory variable, causal distance, and mechanism.

Mahalanobis distance.   Measure of the distance between two cases/observations based on their values of multiple variables.

Matching.   A quantitative method to identify comparable cases (or groups of cases) for comparison. In our context used as a way to choose cases for comparative analysis of pathways.

Measurement validity.   The extent to which assigned measures or scores generated by a coding procedure capture the theoretical concept being examined.

Mechanism.   Unobserved factors that lie between an explanatory variable and outcome in a causal chain. They are analogous to mediating or intervening variables that can, at least in theory, be manipulated. See also causal distance.

Mixed-method research.   The use of both large-N and small-N research approaches in a single project or study.

Multi-method research.   See mixed-method research.

Multiple causal pathways.   See equifinality.

Pathway analysis.   A mode of research that focuses on understanding the connections(s) between a causal variable and an outcome across different cases (as opposed to focusing on explaining a singular event or case). Pathway analysis ultimately has two goals: (1) to gain insight into mechanisms connecting some explanatory variable, X1, and some outcome, Y, in specific cases; and (2) to use insights from these cases to generate hypotheses about mechanisms in the unstudied population of cases that feature the X1/Y relationship. See also comparative pathway analysis.

Process tracing.   A method that seeks to identify intervening causal processes between an explanatory variable (X1) and the dependent variable (Y) or outcome to be explained.

Reliability.   The consistency of a measure over replications of a coding procedure.

Residual.   The difference between an observed value of a variable and the value predicted by the statistical model.

Residual-based case selection.   A mode of case selection for pathway analysis which directs researchers to seek cases that (1) are not outliers (or at least extreme outliers) in the full regression model and where (2) the X1 variable is related to the outcome Y. To assess these criteria, researchers analyze the residuals of individual cases in the model after estimating a regression.

Scenarios 1–4.   Four paradigmatic relationships between X1 and Y: Scenario 1 (Single Pathway Scenario or cases where there is single mechanism and single path connecting X1 and Y); Scenario 2 (Direct and Indirect Pathways Scenario or cases where there is a single mechanism but multiple paths (i.e., direct and indirect effects) connecting X1 and Y); Scenario 3 (Multiple Exclusive Pathways Scenario or cases with multiple, exclusive mechanisms and multiple paths); and Scenario 4 (Multiple Non-Exclusive Pathways Scenario or cases with multiple, non-exclusive mechanisms and multiple paths connecting X1 and Y). See Table 2.2 and related text for more detail.

Sensitivity analysis.   A technique to understand how changes made in statistical analysis affect the conclusions we reach. In the study of causal mechanisms, it typically refers to analyzing how changes in the correlation between the key explanatory variable and the mechanism(s) would affect our estimates of the effect of both the explanatory variable and the mechanism(s).

Sequential ignorability.   An analytic requirement for large-N studies that seek to estimate the effect of a mechanism, which requires researchers to disentangle mechanisms from each other and from the treatment so that we can estimate the independent effect of the mechanism(s).

Variable-based case selection.   A mode of case selection for pathway analysis which directs researchers to seek cases with extreme values of X1 and Y.

Variation in case characteristics.   One of two factors in determining case selection for pathway analysis, which means the extent to which the cases selected vary in terms of the X1/Y relationship, the X values and the Y values.

Within-case comparisons.   Analysis of observations within a single case, such as observations within the same country at different time periods or at different geographic sub-regions.

References

Achen, Christopher H. 1986. *The Statistical Analysis of Quasi-Experiments.* Berkeley, CA: University of California Press.

Adler, Nancy E. and Judith Stewart. 2010. "Health Disparities Across the Lifespan: Meaning, Methods, and Mechanisms." *Annals of the New York Academy of Sciences: The Biology of Disadvantage* 1186: 5–23.

Angrist, Joshua D. and Jörn-Steffen Pischke. 2009. *Mostly Harmless Econometrics: An Empiricist Companion.* Princeton University Press.

Baron, Reuben M. and David A. Kenny. 1986. "The Moderator–Mediator Variable Distinction in Social Psychological Research: Conceptual, Strategic, and Statistical Considerations." *Journal of Personality and Social Psychology* 51(6): 1173–82.

Baum, Lawrence. 1997. *The Puzzle of Judicial Behavior.* Ann Arbor, MI: University of Michigan Press.

2006. *Judges and Their Audiences: A Perspective on Judicial Behavior.* Princeton University Press.

Beck, Nathaniel, Jonathan N. Katz, and Richard Tucker. 1998. "Taking Time Seriously: Time-Series-Cross-Section Analysis with a Binary Dependent Variable." *American Journal of Political Science* 42(4): 1260–88.

Bennett, Andrew. 2010. "Process Tracing and Causal Inference." In *Rethinking Causal Inference: Diverse Tools, Shared Standards*, ed. Henry Brady and David Collier. 2nd edition. Lanham, MD: Rowman & Littlefield, 207–21.

Berry, Frances S. and William D. Berry. 1990. "State Lottery Adoptions as Policy Innovations: An Event History Analysis." *American Political Science Review* 84(2): 395–415.

Brady, Henry E. and David Collier, eds. 2004. *Rethinking Social Inquiry: Diverse Tools, Shared Standards.* New York: Rowman & Littlefield.

eds. 2010. *Rethinking Social Inquiry: Diverse Tools, Shared Standards.* 2nd edition. New York: Rowman & Littlefield.

Burton, Steven J. 1992. *Judging in Good Faith.* Cambridge University Press.

Cartwright, Nancy and Jeremy Hardie. 2012. *Evidence-Based Policy: A Practical Guide to Doing It Better.* New York: Oxford University Press.

Chapin, Charles. 1924. "Deaths among Taxpayers and Non-Taxpayers, Income Tax, Providence, 1865." *American Journal of Public Health* 14(8): 647–51.

Chatfield, Chris. 1995. "Model Uncertainty, Data Mining, and Statistical Inference." *Journal of Royal Statistical Society, Series A (Statistics in Society)* 158(3): 419–66.

Collier, David. 2011. "Understanding Process Tracing." *PS: Political Science & Politics* 44(4): 823–30.

Collier, David, Henry E. Brady, and Jason Seawright. 2004. "Sources of Leverage in Causal Inference: Toward an Alternative View of Methodology." In *Rethinking Causal Inference: Diverse Tools, Shared Standards*, ed. Henry Brady and David Collier. 2nd edition. Lanham: Rowman & Littlefield, 229–66.

Collier, Paul and Anke Hoeffler. 2004. "Greed and Grievance in Civil War." *Oxford Economic Papers* 56(4): 563–95.

Coombs, Lolagene C. 1941. "Economic Differentials in Causes of Death." *Medical Care* 1: 246–55.

Cushman, Barry. 1998. *Rethinking the New Deal Court: The Structure of a Constitutional Revolution.* New York: Oxford University Press.

Deaton, Angus. 2002. "Policy Implications of the Gradient of Health and Wealth." *Health Affairs* 21(2): 13–30.

Dworkin, Ronald. 1978. *Taking Rights Seriously.* Cambridge, MA: Harvard University Press.

Elster, Jon. 2007. *Explaining Social Behavior: More Nuts and Bolts for the Social Sciences.* New York: Cambridge University Press.

Epstein, Lee, William M. Landes, and Richard A. Posner. 2013. *The Behavior of Federal Judges: A Theoretical & Empirical Study.* Cambridge, MA: Harvard University Press.

Fearon, James D. 1995. "Rationalist Explanations for War." *International Organization* 49(3): 379–414.

Freedman, David A. 1991. "Statistical Models and Shoe Leather." *Sociological Methodology* 21: 291–313.

Freese, Jeremy and Karen E. Lutfey. 2011. "Fundamental Causality: Challenges of an Animating Concept for Medical Sociology." In *Handbook of Medical Sociology*, ed. B. Pescosolido, J. Martin, J. McLeod, and A. Rogers. New York: Springer, 67–81.

Geddes, Barbara. 1990. "How the Cases You Choose Affect the Answers You Get: Selection Bias in Comparative Politics." *Political Analysis* 2(1): 131–50.

Geertz, Clifford. 1973. "Thick Description: Toward an Interpretive Theory of Culture." In *The Interpretation of Cultures*. New York: Basic Books, 3–30.

George, Alexander L. and Andrew Bennett. 2005. *Case Studies and Theory Development in the Social Sciences*. Cambridge, MA: MIT Press.

Gerber, Alan, Donald Green, and Edward Kaplan. 2004. "The Illusion of Learning from Observational Data." In *Problems and Methods in the Study of Politics*, ed. Ian Shapiro, Rogers Smith, and Tarek Masoud. Cambridge University Press, 251–73.

Gerring, John. 2004. "What Is a Case Study and What Is It Good For?" *American Political Science Review* 98(2): 341–54.

2007. *Case Study Research: Principles and Practices*. New York: Cambridge University Press.

2008. "The Mechanismic Worldview: Thinking Inside the Box." *British Journal of Political Science* 38(1): 161–79.

2010. "Causal Mechanisms: Yes, But . . . " *Comparative Political Studies* 43(11): 1499–526.

2012. *Social Science Methodology: A Unified Framework*. 2nd edition. Cambridge University Press.

Gillman, Howard. 1993. *The Constitution Besieged: The Rise and Demise of Lochner Era Police Powers Jurisprudence*. Durham, NC: Duke University Press.

1996. "More on the Origins of the Fuller Court's Jurisprudence: The Scope of Federal Power over Commerce and Manufacturing in Nineteenth-Century Constitutional Law." *Political Research Quarterly* 49: 415–37.

2001. *The Votes that Counted: How the Court Decided the 2000 Presidential Election*. University of Chicago Press.

Glynn, Adam N. and Nahomi Ichino. 2012. "Increasing Inferential Leverage in the Comparative Method: Placebo Tests in Small-n Research." October version. Available at http://people.fas.harvard.edu/~nichino/

Gray, Virginia. 1973. "Innovation in the States: A Diffusion Study." *American Political Science Review* 67(4): 1174–85.

1994. "Competition, Emulation, and Policy Innovation." In *New Perspectives on American Politics*, ed. L. Dodd and C. Jillson. Washington, DC: CQ Press, 230–48.

Gu, Xing S. and Paul R. Rosenbaum. 1993. "Comparison of Multivariate Matching Methods: Structures, Distances, and Algorithms." *Journal of Computational and Graphical Statistics* 2(4): 405–20.

Heckman, James J. and Jeffrey A. Smith. 1995. "Assessing the Case for Social Experiments." *Journal of Economic Perspectives* 9(2): 85–110.

Hedstrom, Peter. 2005. *Dissecting the Social: On the Principles of Analytical Sociology.* Cambridge University Press.

Hedstrom, Peter and Petri Ylikoski. 2010. "Causal Mechanisms in the Social Sciences." *Annual Review of Sociology* 36: 49–67.

Ho, Daniel E., Kosuke Imai, Gary King, and Elizabeth A. Stuart. 2007. "Matching as Nonparametric Preprocessing for Reducing Model Dependence in Parametric Causal Inference." *Political Analysis* 15(3): 199–236.

Imai, Kosuke, Luke Keele, and Dustin Tingley. 2010. "A General Approach to Causal Mediation Analysis." *Psychological Methods* (15)4: 309–34.

Imai, Kosuke, Luke Keele, Dustin Tingley, and Teppei Yamamoto. 2011. "Unpacking the Black Box of Causality: Learning about Causal Mechanisms from Experimental and Observational Studies." *American Political Science Review* 105(4): 765–89.

Imai, Kosuke, Dustin Tingley, and Teppei Yamamoto. 2013. "Experimental Designs for Identifying Causal Mechanisms." *Journal of the Royal Statistical Society* A 176, Part 1: 5–51.

Imai, Kosuke and Teppei Yamamoto. 2013. "Identification and Sensitivity Analysis for Multiple Causal Mechanisms: Revisiting Evidence from Framing Experiments." *Political Analysis* 21(2): 141–71.

Kantor, David. 2006. "MAHAPICK: Stata Module to Select Matching Observation Based on a Mahalanobis Distance Measure." Statistical Software Components S456703, Boston College Department of Economics, revised November 15, 2012.

King, Gary, Robert O. Keohane, and Sidney Verba. 1994. *Designing Social Inquiry: Scientific Inference in Qualitative Research.* Princeton University Press.

Kiser, Edgar and Michael Hechter. 1991. "The Role of General Theory in Comparative-Historical Sociology." *American Journal of Sociology* 97(1): 1–30.

Kittel, Bernhard and Hannes Winner. 2005. "How Reliable Is Pooled Analysis in Political Economy? The Globalization–Welfare State Nexus Revisited." *European Journal of Political Research* 44(2): 269–93.

Link, Bruce G. and Jo Phelan. 1995. "Social Conditions as Fundamental Causes of Disease." *Journal of Health and Social Behavior* (Extra Issue) 35: 80–94.

——. 1996. "Understanding Sociodemographic Differences in Health: The Role of Fundamental Social Causes." *American Journal of Public Health* 86(4): 471–73.

——. 2002. "McKeown and the Idea that Social Conditions are the Fundamental Causes of Disease." *American Journal of Public Health* 92(5): 730–32.

——. 2005. "Fundamental Sources of Health Inequalities." In *Policy Challenges in Modern Health Care*, ed. David Mechanic, Lynn B. Rogut, David C. Colby, and James R. Knickman. New Brunswick, NJ: Rutgers University Press, 71–84.

Lu, Bo, Robert Greevy, Xinyi Xu, and Cole Beck. 2011. "Optimal Nonbipartite Matching and Its Statistical Applications." *American Statistician* 65(1): 21–30.

Lutfey, Karen and Jeremy Freese. 2005. "Toward Some Fundamentals of Fundamental Causality: Socioeconomic Status and Health in the Routine Clinic Visit for Diabetes." *American Journal of Sociology* 110(5): 1326–72.

Mahoney, James and Gary Goertz. 2006. "A Tale of Two Cultures: Contrasting Quantitative and Qualitative Research." *Political Analysis* 14(3): 227–49.

Malhotra, Neil and Jon A. Krosnick. 2007. "The Effect of Survey Mode and Sampling on Inferences about Political Attitudes and Behavior: Comparing the 2000 and 2004 ANES to Internet Surveys with Nonprobability Samples." *Political Analysis* 15: 286–323.

Marmot, Michael G. 2004. *The Status Syndrome: How Social Standing Affects Our Health and Longevity*. New York: Holt Paperbacks.

Marmot, Michael G. and Martin J. Shipley. 1996. "Do Socioeconomic Differences in Mortality Persist after Retirement? 25 Year Follow Up of Civil Servants from the First Whitehall Study." *British Medical Journal* 313(7066): 1177–80.

Marmot, Michael G., Martin J. Shipley, and Geoffrey Rose. 1984. "Inequalities in Death: Specific Explanations of a General Pattern?" *The Lancet* 323(8384): 1003–06.

Mayntz, Renate. 2004. "Mechanisms in the Analysis of Social Macro-Phenomena." *Philosophy of the Social Sciences* 34(2): 237–59.

Meara, Ellen R., Seth Richards, and David M. Cutler. 2008. "The Gap Gets Bigger: Changes in Mortality and Life Expectancy, by Education, 1981–2000." *Health Affairs* 27(2): 350–60.

Mechanic, David. 2000. "Rediscovering the Social Determinants of Health." *Health Affairs* 19(3): 3269–76.

2002. "Disadvantage, Inequality, and Social Policy." *Health Affairs* 21(2): 48–59.

Nielsen, Richard. 2014. "Case Selection Via Matching." Unpublished manuscript. Last version revised January 31, 2014. Available at www.mit.edu/~rnielsen/research.htm

Norkus, Zenonas. 2004. "Mechanism as Miracle Makers? The Rise and Inconsistencies of the 'Mechanismic Approach' in Social Science and History." *History and Theory* 44(3): 348–72.

Pappas, Gregory, Susan Queen, Wilbur Hadden, and Gail Fisher. 1993. "The Increasing Disparity in Mortality between Socioeconomic Groups in the United States, 1960 and 1986." *New England Journal of Medicine* 329(2): 103–09.

Pearl, Judea. 2009. *Causality: Models, Reasoning, and Inference.* 2nd edition. Cambridge University Press.

Pritchett, C. Herman. 1948. *The Roosevelt Court.* New York: Macmillan.

Ragin, Charles. 2000. *Fuzzy Set Social Science.* University of Chicago Press.

Rohde, David W. and Harold J. Spaeth. 1976. *Supreme Court Decision Making.* San Francisco, CA: Freeman.

Rosenbaum, Paul R. and Donald B. Rubin. 1983. "The Central Role of the Propensity Score in Observational Studies for Causal Effects." *Biometrika* 70(1): 41–55.

1984. "Reducing Bias in Observational Studies Using Subclassification on the Propensity Score." *Journal of the American Statistical Association* 79(387): 516–24.

Rosenbaum, Paul R. and Jeffrey H. Silber. 2001. "Matching and Thick Description in an Observational Study of Mortality after Surgery." *Biostatistics* 2(2): 217–32.

Ross, Michael L. 2004. "How Do Natural Resources Influence Civil War? Evidence from Thirteen Cases." *International Organization* 58(1): 35–67.

Rubin, Donald B. 2006. *Matched Sampling for Causal Effects.* Cambridge University Press.

2008. "For Objective Causal Inference, Design Trumps Analysis." *Annals of Applied Statistics* 2(3): 808–40.

Rubin, Donald B. and Neal Thomas. 2000. "Combining Propensity Score Matching with Additional Adjustments for Prognostic Covariates." *Journal of the American Statistical Association* 95(45): 573–85.

Schubert, Glendon. 1965. *The Judicial Mind: The Attitudes and Ideologies of Supreme Court Justices 1946–1963.* Evanston, IL: Northwestern University Press.

Seawright, Jason and John Gerring. 2008. "Case Selection Techniques in Case Study Research: A Menu of Qualitative and Quantitative Options." *Political Research Quarterly* 61(2): 294–308.

Segal, Jeffrey A., Charles M. Cameron, and Donald R. Songer. 1995. "Decision Making on the U.S. Courts of Appeals." In *Contemplating Courts,* ed. Lee Epstein. Washington, DC: CQ Press, 227–46.

Segal, Jeffrey A. and Albert D. Cover. 1989. "Ideological Values and Votes of U.S. Supreme Court Justices." *American Political Science Review* 83: 557–65.

Segal, Jeffrey A. and Harold J. Spaeth. 1993. *The Supreme Court and the Attitudinal Model.* New York: Cambridge University Press.

2002. *The Supreme Court and the Attitudinal Model Revisited.* New York: Cambridge University Press.

Simmons, Beth A., Frank Dobbin, and Geoffrey Garrett. 2006. "Introduction: The International Diffusion of Liberalism." *International Organization* 60(3): 781–810.

2008. *The Global Diffusion of Markets and Democracy.* New York: Cambridge University Press.

Simmons, Beth A. and Zachary Elkins. 2004. "The Globalization of Liberalization: Policy Diffusion in the International Political Economy." *American Political Science Review* 98(1): 171–90.

Spaeth, Harold J. and Jeffrey A. Segal. 1999. *Majority Rule or Minority Will: Adherence to Precedent on the U.S. Supreme Court.* New York: Cambridge University Press.

Stuart, Elizabeth A. and Donald B. Rubin. 2007. "Best Practices in Quasi-Experimental Designs: Matching Methods for Causal Inference." In *Best Practices in Quantitative Social Science,* ed. J. Osborne. Thousand Oaks, CA: Sage Publications, 155–76.

Volden, Craig, Michael M. Ting, and Daniel P. Carpenter. 2008. "A Formal Model of Learning and Policy Diffusion." *American Political Science Review* 102(3): 319–32.

Waldner, David. 2007. "Transforming Inferences into Explanations: Lessons from the Study of Mass Extinctions." In *Theory and Evidence in Comparative Politics and International Relations,* ed. R. N. Lebow and M. I. Lichbach. New York: Palgrave Macmillan, 145–76.

2012. "Process Tracing and Causal Mechanisms." In *The Oxford Handbook of Philosophy and Social Science,* ed. Harold Kinkaid. New York: Oxford University Press, 65–84.

Winship, Christopher and Michael Sobel. 2004. "Causal Inference in Sociological Studies." In *Handbook of Data Analysis,* ed. Melissa A. Hardy and Alan Bryman. Thousand Oaks, CA: Sage Publications, 481–503.

Index